Directive
Group Therapy

INNOVATIVE MENTAL HEALTH TREATMENT

SLACK Incorpora... ...ofare, Ne... ...08086

Dedicated to Gram,
who has always believed in me.

Printed in the United States of America

Library of Congress Catalog Card Number: 88-042754

ISBN: 1-55642-050-1

Published by: SLACK Incorporated
              6900 Grove Rd.
              Thorofare, NJ 08086

Last digit is print number: 10   9   8   7   6   5   4   3   2   1

Table of Contents

Foreword

Directive Group Therapy: Innovative Mental Health Treatment is a book that will make a difference. When Kathy Kaplan started Directive Group at The George Washington University Medical Center, she was breaking new ground. The concepts and practical guidance that make her new book such a valuable resource were just beginning to emerge. The result of her insight and hard work is a discrete, theoretically and clinically sound group therapy for minimally functioning patients. *Directive Group Therapy* makes this integrated approach to treatment, and the many lessons learned during its genesis and evolution, available to a wide audience of mental health care professionals. In turn, many more patients will benefit from a service designed for their special needs.

A central tenet of *Directive Group Therapy* is that therapists must be willing to take risks — informed, planned ones to be sure. What we know about the theory of therapy often bears little relationship to practice when we implement from the drawing board to the real world. Kathy points out in a personal, constructive way that it is all right to have failures, to learn from them, and to modify approaches and procedures, or even to change the underlying rationale for action. By doing so, both therapist and patient alike grow.

It helps to think about the establishment of new groups as a challenge — the excitement of creation. Among other things, it is also a staff political problem. *Directive Group Therapy* addresses the issues of diplomacy in gaining support from other staff on the ward in order to make a new initiative in therapy a viable concern. There is often frank skepticism about what other disciplines have to offer. One of Kathy's contributions is to emphasize the roles the group leader must play as educator and change agent in a delicate situtation.

In this regard, the key supporter is the ward director, whose active engagement is a very effective way of garnering the resources necessary to promote a Directive Group, as well as other therapies. I was proud to be ward director and provide both administrative and clinical support for Kathy's ideas to become a reality.

Kathy Kaplan is an exceedingly talented and creative individual. I can attest to this first hand, having worked with her for years as co-leader and colleague. She is too modest in her book, but others, including Irwin Yalom, in his book *Inpatient Group Psychotherapy*, pay proper tribute to her as the architect of our group therapy program. I think it is a credit to Kathy's vision and competence that the Directive Group continues to thrive long after she has left our inpatient service. I fully expect that many professionals will go beyond this book, research the group, and strike out in new directions. If that happens, I suspect that both Kathy and I will consider this work a great success.

Marc Hertzman, M.D., Director, Hospital Services

Department of Psychiatry, The George Washington University Medical Center

Author: Inpatient Psychiatry: Toward Rapid Restoration of Function, NY: Human Services Press, 1984.

Preface

Directive Group Therapy: Innovative Mental Health Treatment is a response to the many requests I have received from students, new practitioners, and experienced clinicians in mental health settings who have asked for more information on how to lead Directive Group, a short-term therapy designed for minimally functioning patients. While most acute care psychiatric settings offer a wide range of group therapies, many lack an effective group treatment for the most disorganized, disturbed, and dependent patients on the unit.

This book describes a specialized approach for dealing with such patients. People with similar severe functional problems due to neurologic disorders, mental retardation, or chronicity may also benefit from this form of group treatment. Therefore, this book is applicable in long-term inpatient settings, community programs, and nursing homes. Although this group was developed from an occupational therapy perspective, it has always had interdisciplinary collaboration. Any mental health professional involved in leading groups can use this book as a resource — nurses, psychologists, social workers, counselors, therapeutic recreation specialists, occupational therapists and assistants, and mental health technicians.

To lead Directive Group effectively, minimal qualifications of the leaders require some academic preparation in group theory and practice, personal experience as part of a training group, and supervision with an experienced group therapist while leading a treatment group. Students or staff who do not meet these qualifications can learn a great deal and provide a valuable service by apprenticing as leaders. Success in leading this group additionally depends on acquiring the knowledge to understand processes for helping individuals and groups change.

My experience with occupational therapy personnel, fieldwork interns, and students in the classroom has convinced me that they have a need to learn more effectively how to apply group process principles to the clinical setting. Students have voiced their difficulty bridging theory and practice. Interns have confided they were uncertain how to select activities for different level groups and didn't know what to do when the group just didn't click. Clinicians have complained they had problems getting their group to be supported by the staff.

Directive Group is an example of how to apply group dynamics to a particular patient population and practice setting. The Directive Group can also provide a process for professional accountability through evaluating program effectiveness. This book not only addresses what Directive Group is and how to lead it, but also how to look at the broader issues surrounding its place in a group therapy program.

This book is a personal book based on my experiences learning to be a health care professional. My awareness of my own process of development has helped me be more sensitive to those needs in others. I wrote this as if I were in conversation with you, much as I do when consulting with occupational therapy personnel and students. While reading, consider this a chance to talk with someone about what it's really like to do what you do. At its most fundamental level the book offers four remedies for surviving the stresses of working with therapy groups day in and day out:

-Prepare yourself with the knowledge, skills, and realistic self-assessment necessary for your practice area.

-Learn to offer a needed service very well.

-Innovate through interdisciplinary program development.

-Develop yourself through understanding the sources of your own anxiety and finding ways to deal with them effectively.

To get the most from this book, I suggest reading each chapter sequentially to be familiar with the overall content. Those interested in establishing and leading a Directive Group can then go back to Chapters 2 through 8 for reference and use the Appendix for activity ideas. Supervisors may find it useful to assign Chapters 1 and 12 to students and interns who need to learn more about preparing themselves for group leadership and coping with their anxiety from being a new group leader. Chapters 9, 10, and 11 form a unit on innovating for program development and include material on change processes, systems thinking, and ward politics.

Introduction

Think of mental health treatment and you think of groups — activity groups, verbal groups, traditional psychotherapy groups, informal groups, large groups, family therapy groups, cooking groups. Most health care professionals have some background in group work; yet the extent and emphasis varies considerably. Group work or group therapy, as used in this book, refers globally to the many forms of treatment provided in a group setting, such as those listed above. Inpatient and community settings offer many opportunities for participating in leading groups. Even physical rehabilitation departments are increasingly using groups to augment treatment for patients who have suffered a stroke, spinal cord injury, back pain, or traumatic brain injury.

Based on my experiences establishing and developing an occupational therapy program for short-term psychiatric inpatients, I am sensitive to how much time it takes to create materials for new groups. I remember having to document the purpose and scope of the program, policies and procedures, descriptions of evaluation and treatment methods, individual evaluation results, weekly progress notes, AND handouts for specific group sessions. I wished I had more resources readily available so that I could have spent less time in preparation and more in patient treatment.

I believe many clinicians and students share these concerns. They are aware that the competition in the current health care marketplace requires documentation of the benefits of treatment. New reimbursement policies, such as the three-hour-per-day therapy criterion by Medicare, also put increasing demands on therapists for productivity. Group treatment is one likely response to this requirement. At the same time, evidence of quality programs must be provided, including ways to predict the effectiveness of treatment groups of various purposes and strategies. Therefore, the less time that is spent "recreating the wheel," the more energy will be available for program development and accountability.

Ultimately, research will give us more knowledge about the distinguishing features of specific group techniques. Such research will depend on the clarification of conceptual issues, such as what types of groups benefit which types of patients. Detailed descriptions of groups, such as the one offered here, build consistent treatment approaches which can then be compared through research protocols.

This book is a practical resource for leading the Directive Group. By offering specific activity suggestions, it provides practitioners new to leading this group with a repertoire of resources. New leaders are then freer to focus on identifying patients' needs, reflecting on the group dynamics, and intervening effectively. As the material becomes familiar, group leaders are then assisted in adapting these ideas to their special situations, settings, and styles.

The manual begins with a discussion of the knowledge required to be an effective group leader. It refers the reader to primary source material for gaining additional background. Chapter 1 gives reassurance to the fledgling therapist and suggests a context for learning new skills and attitudes.

Chapter 2 describes the Directive Group, providing the reader with a common base necessary for understanding the remaining chapters. The components, setting, and theoretical orientation of the group are discussed. Setting the stage for later adaptations, this chapter enumerates the principles that embody the essence of the group.

Chapter 3 gives a framework for identifying the type of individuals who could benefit from such a treatment program. By doing a basic needs assessment, therapists can begin to clarify just who needs Directive Group and why, and what kind of service to offer to meet those needs and document progress. A case example traces a patient from admission to the hospital to discharge from Directive Group.

Chapter 4 goes into detail about how to structure the Directive Group, offering guidelines for planning the group and a rationale for the sequence of events. Specific activity suggestions are given which have proved useful over the years. The Appendix contains many more activity ideas.

The necessity for group goals and the relation of Directive Group to the other groups in the inpatient program lead to Chapter 5. How the four group goals are operationalized is clarified through a case example.

Chapter 6 describes how to use ten common goals to individualize patient needs. Goals help reduce patient resistance and increase active participation. The value of weekly goal-identification meetings, which foster creativity and promote collaboration among group co-leaders, is also discussed.

Chapter 7 emphasizes the roles of the leaders. In particular, the relationships developed in Directive Groups occur within the context of play. This arena needs to be understood and created by the leaders in order to give the patients the degree of support and involvement they need. The ways in which the leaders are role models for action and interaction are explained. In addition the importance of offering choices is examined.

Adapting activities on the spot is a hallmark of Directive Group. Because it is so difficult to predict responses with patients functioning at a minimal level, guidelines are given to adapt activities. There are ways to change the task and there are ways to change the process. Both are explored in Chapter 8.

Just as patients differ, so too do the settings in which treatment programs occur. Chapter 9 talks about how to adapt Directive Group to your facility. Addressing resistance to change, attention is directed toward norms, the physical environment, staffing, and the patient population.

For those involved in program development, Chapters 10 and 11 are resources. Chapter 10 provides a way to conceptualize the interdisciplinary program as a system and offers a personal perspective on professional growth. Different approaches are needed for new or revised programs. General guidelines are given for making system changes and identifying program needs. Chapter 11 gets more specific about introducing change into the system and considering the ward politics. It contains practical advice for brainstorming about a current program and structuring the new one.

Making use of the ideas in this book requires not only conceptual integration, but emotional perspective as well. We come full circle in Chapter 12 from the first chapter in which the new leader asks, Who Me? Now we say, Yes You, but with the knowledge that no matter how much skill and experience a clinician has, he or she still will always deal with ongoing anxiety. This chapter explores some typical dilemmas and ways of using them to enhance professional and personal development.

Supervisors and educators shun the thought of a "cook book" approach to practice. Yet, students and mental health personnel sometimes long for something more — some book or piece of advice that helps them decide what to do in their situation. Perhaps everyone is concerned with the same issue: How to develop clinical judgment. I think a deeper look at the process of cooking provides a clue, serving as a metaphor for the process of learning to lead groups.

I like to think of this book as a cook book in the best sense of the term. The advantage of the cook book is that it provides the novice cook with reliable recipes which will be successful if the steps are followed. People have only to remember the first time they tried to boil an egg or when (and how!) they learned the difference between a garlic clove and a garlic bulb, to realize how many skills, techniques, and tools are required even for basic meal preparation.

Through practice and experience, anyone can learn to cook. James Beard, in his book *The Theory and Practice of Good Cooking*[1] says that the more people know about cooking, the more fun it is. "As a student absorbs the answers to all these continual questions, his understanding deepens and is reflected in the more experienced way he uses his cooking hands, can tell by touch when something is done to perfection, can identify flavors and compare dishes, knows exactly what to do at the market. At that point the student is on his own. He no longer needs to follow slavishly a set recipe; he can rely on his own skills — his taste memory, the understanding he has gained of techniques, flavorings, and food combinations — and build on his knowledge."

Just as learning to cook is clearly a developmental process, so is learning to lead therapy groups. First one needs a background of normal behavior in order appreciate the pathological. Then one needs to understand group dynamics before applying the principles to special populations and settings. Throughout, one needs to be open to the process of self-awareness in order to more fully form helping relationships.

Likewise, as cooking relies on special equipment arranged in a kitchen, so too does leading a group require appropriate objects and a therapeutic environment. Learning basic recipes is much like learning basic activities. As one develops skill and judgment, one can alter a recipe to accommodate seasonal foods, special diets, or a missing ingredient. Yet, not even for the most experienced are all recipes or activities fail-safe — flexibility is a must. When one is leading an activity, one can also adapt the activity to meet the energy level of the group, the special interests of some members, or a lack in some of the supplies.

According to Julia Child,[2] "Cooking, thank heaven, is not a vast jumble of recipe after recipe, each different, all to be learned. A cooking repertoire is, in fact, like a great family of parents and cousins — relatives of all sorts — in which foods of a similar nature are usually begun in the same way....once you've made a dish, store it and any of its related family parts in your mental cuisine computer. Call any or all of it up again when you are casting about for ideas. The more you cook, the more you'll have in that bank. That's how all those fabled experienced cooks' got their reputations."

The readers of this book will find themselves in a similar process of developing their therapeutic repertoire as they learn to apply the information to their own settings. What may first appear as an isolated activity soon becomes a prototype for a special type of group need. Ways to identify goals for one patient soon lead to adapting goals to meet the special needs of many individuals. The practitioner may suddenly realize, when faced with an unexpected group response, that he or she quickly thought of several alternatives and confidently chose one which worked quite well.

The term "clinical practice" aptly describes the daily opportunities afforded the clinician who leads groups as part of an occupational therapy or other group therapy program for a given patient population. Excitement from involvement in this continuous learning process comes when experience gives rise to mastery, confidence leads to greater satisfaction, and success stimulates innovation. *Directive Group Therapy: Innovative Mental Health Treatment* can help launch you on this important developmental journey.

References

1. Beard, J (1977). Theory and Practice of Good Cooking. New York: Alfred A. Knopf.
2. Child, J (1984, September 23). From Julia Child's Kitchen. Parade Magazine.

Suggested Readings

Ducombe, L (1985). Group work in occupational therapy: A survey of practice. American Journal of Occupational Therapy., 39, 163-170.

Intagliata, S & Hollander, R (1987). The 3-hour therapy criterion: A challenge for rehabilitation facilities. American Journal of Occupational Therapy, 41(5), 297-304.

Johnson, J (1983). The changing medical marketplace as a context for the practice of occupational therapy. Health Through Occupation: Theory and Practice in Occupational Therapy. Philadelphia: FA Davis (pp. 295-309).

Parloff, M & Dies, R (1977). Group psychotherapy outcome research. International Journal of Group Psychotherapy. 27, 281-319.

Yalom I (1983). Inpatient Group Psychotherapy. New York. Basic Books.

Acknowledgments

Writing this book is my way of thanking many of the people who have supported me in my professional development. While this book is not necessarily for them, it is largely because of them. In particular, I want to acknowledge the longstanding support I have been given by my husband, Colburn T. Cherney, to forge ahead with my many projects, even when they kept me from spending as much time with him as we would have liked. I also could not have developed the Directive Group without the collaboration and commitment of Marc Hertzman, M.D., the director of the Inpatient Program at The George Washington University Medical Center (GWUMC). He believed in me and my ideas and gave me lots of room to take risks and grow. I want to express gratitude to Gary Kielhofner, Dr.P.H., O.T.R., F.A.O.T.A., who throughout my masters degree program helped me rethink my ideas on Directive Group in terms of the model of human occupation. I also want to thank my doctoral program advisor, Jerry Harvey, Ph.D., for helping me learn so much about anxiety, change, and relationships.

I also appreciate the time and expertise four colleagues and friends gave to review and help shape the original manuscript: Sandra Cohen, M.A., O.T.R., currently the director of an expressive therapy department, who used to lead Directive Group after I had left GWUMC, and helped examine the activity ideas in the Appendix; Curtis Cook, Ph.D., C.P.C.M., a fellow doctoral student who offered a nonoccupational therapy perspective on the organization of the book and did copy editing; Debbie Frum, M.Ed., O.T.R., formally a staff member at the American Occupational Therapy Association when I consulted there, and currently chief of occupational therapy at a large community hospital, who looked at the manual for theoretical, technical, and stylistic consistency; and Jan Magruder, O.T.R., leader of Directive Group under my supervision as a student, and now a clinician with brain-injured adults, who had suggestions for application of the group to other settings and populations and for helping students and practitioners feel comfortable making the transition to group leader.

Finally, I want to thank all the people at SLACK who were involved in the publication of this book. In particular, Harry Benson's enthusiasm and leadership, as the Editorial Director, made meeting our deadlines possible. Lynn Borders' persistence and flexibility, in her role as Associate Editor, transformed the manuscript into its final form. They involved four reviewers in an exciting collaboration. I am most grateful for the excellent suggestions and dedication of Ellen Kolodner, M.S.S., O.T.R./L., F.A.O.T.A., assistant professor and fieldwork coordinator at Thomas Jefferson University; Diane Hawkins, C.O.T.A./L., group dynamics specialist at The Sheppard and Enoch Pratt Hospital; Frances Oakley, M.S., O.T.R./L., coordinator of clinical research for the Occupational Therapy Service at The National Institutes of Health; and Sally Ryan, C.O.T.A., R.O.H., instructor at College of St. Catherine, Occupational Therapy Department.

Biography

Kathy Kaplan draws on her rich clinical experience and knowledge gained as an educator, supervisor, program director, consultant, and researcher in writing this book. She has published extensively in the field, including co-editing with Patricia Ostrow the recent American Occupational Therapy Association publication, *Occupational Therapy in Mental Health: A Guide to Outcomes Research.*

Ms. Kaplan received her B.S. in occupational therapy from the University of Wisconsin in 1972 and her advanced masters in occupational therapy from Virginia Commonwealth University in 1983. She is currently a consultant in private practice and a doctoral candidate at The George Washington University in Washington, D.C., where she is furthering her interest and expertise in the underlying processes fundamental to individual and organizational change.

CHAPTER 1

WHO ME?

What the Group Leader Needs to Know

Just as the beginning cook wouldn't attempt to prepare a five-course French gourmet meal for the first dinner party, the novice group leader shouldn't expect to lead the most well orchestrated, sensitive, productive, and meaningful group the first few times. The five-course meal involves integration of so much knowledge to be successful that it is unrealistic to think it could be attempted all at once. That fact is so obvious it is almost laughable. And yet often those who are new to groups put that type of pressure on themselves and can't see the folly in it. Let's examine why.

If you have observed your supervisor leading an exercise group, you probably thought it looked pretty easy to do. The scene goes something like this: The patients are relatively punctual. One offers to help set up the tape player, while two others arrange the chairs in a large circle. There is some animated chatting and expectant glances as if patients are anticipating some fun event. Then the supervisor gives a few opening remarks about the purpose of the group. She welcomes new members. She asks an experienced member to start with a warm-up stretch. Everyone joins in.

Next the supervisor shows a new movement sequence. Everyone tries it. A little laughter. Then the leader suggests how to incorporate the movement into a game. One woman says she doesn't want to. The leader makes a comment that seems to put both that individual and the rest of the group at ease. They start the game. Such fun. You get so caught up in the process of the group that you forget to watch the supervisor. Somehow the game gradually winds down; everyone relaxes with deep breathing to the wonderful music in the background. The supervisor asks questions about the activity, how people felt, what they found themselves thinking about. Patients share their experiences back and forth. A few closing comments and it is time to go. You look at the clock. Yep, right on time. You wonder how she paced things so well. Must be easy, it looked so effortless.

Yes, true skillfulness gives the appearance of grace and ease. But that is because one cannot see all of the mistakes, principles, and experiences that have become integrated in the supervisor and which enable such a fine performance. It is not obvious what constitutes rapport, what facilitates interaction, what allows for an activity to be meaningful, or what enables people to have fun. Nor is it crystal clear just what makes the group therapeutic. How can you be sure just from experiencing the session what the goals were or if they were met? How do you measure effectiveness? Can that feeling of everything working out synergistically really be quantified? And should it be?

The five-course dinner example provides some clues about how to start to see what is involved in a truly effective production. First of all, an individual, such as you, might be inspired to prepare such a meal if you had been served such a masterpiece at a fine restaurant. Let's recreate the scene for a minute. You remember the room was beautiful, yet comfortable. There was a soft glow to the lighting that lent itself to quiet and amiable conversation. The waiter was somehow attentive but not intrusive. He gently made suggestions for the wine and described the specials for the evening with eloquence. He made you feel special, deserving of such refined treatment, and expectant of a wonderful meal. And your expectations were met. Every dish was served graciously, presented artistically. You neither felt rushed nor had to wait for service. The temperature, taste, and texture of the food was just right. You were aware that the meal was not just an event in itself, but that it also created a climate for especially enjoying the company of your friend.

When you thought about having a dinner party, it was to recreate the ambience and special quality of that evening. Yet, when you thought about how you could do it, the complexity of the reminiscence revealed itself. First you realized how much planning was involved. You needed to choose recipes that met certain criteria: foods everyone liked, ingredients that were seasonally available, and tastes that seemed balanced. Then you had to think about how much time you had to prepare the food, how long each dish took, and if you had enough burners, pans, and serving platters to coordinate all the steps so that they could be served in sequence. Your past level of cooking skills entered into making decisions about which recipes were not so difficult or lengthy as to impinge on your energy or eventual enjoyment of the meal.

Suddenly you realized something which was taken for granted at the time. The restaurant meal was really a group effort. It took place in the context of a well organized system which relied on various people behind the scenes taking care of many of the factors you now had to do alone. You were going to have to set the table, clean the house, cook and at the same time keep the kitchen in some degree of order, and still have time to get dressed and greet your guests feeling relaxed and in a good humor. Now you could more fully understand the high cost of the restaurant meal.

Occupational therapy therapists and assistants, and other health care personnel who use activities in their treatment, are very familiar with analyzing activities such as this gourmet meal. Because occupational therapy personnel work with the common everyday activities which occupy a wide range of each individual's time and attention, they are well aware of the frequent misperception that occupational therapy treatment is easy and fun to do. The notion comes in part from the observer noting that the activities performed are common — that anyone can do them. Also, some people have such cerebral jobs that they associate concrete activities with play and thus not as serious, important, or valuable as verbal discussion or real work. Even experienced clinicians who use mostly individual treatment or rely on verbal methods of group therapy initially underestimate what is involved in leading an activity oriented group.

The main reason for each of these perceptions is that the *process* of occupational therapy is not emphasized sufficiently. Just because a task is performed doesn't mean it is the only focus. The emotional needs of the group are also important. Content and process coexist; both require examination. When the content involves an activity, however, frequently the complexity of the situation is misperceived. Of course, resistance is found by professionals leading a range of groups, from the psychiatrist who explores unconscious sources of conflict, to the social worker who looks at family dynamics, or the art therapist who uses media to interpret behavior. Effective use of the occupational therapy process involves clarifying the purpose for choosing a particular activity or occupation, exploring the meaning it has to the individuals, understanding the ways in which it affects the relationships in the group, and knowing the rationale for the particular group structure.

Group leaders need to learn to articulate and apply the theory behind their group program, whatever their professional background. They need to convey how the content, structure, and process of the group all interact to create a therapeutic environment. They need to differentiate the criteria for selecting the most appropriate approaches for a given set of individuals — individuals who span a range of levels of functioning and have varying interests and problems. This requires integrating knowledge about therapy, psychiatric problems, and yourself. These topics are important for any group therapy approach and will be addressed in detail for Directive Group in the chapters which follow.

Learning about Group Dynamics

Another topic which is important for understanding group behavior is group dynamics. When you go to the library card catalog and look up "group dynamics," "group theory," or "group counseling," you will be amazed at the number of references on these subjects. The strong and extensive literature on groups comes from many perspectives — sociology, psychology, organizational behavior, education, social work, and psychotherapy — reflecting the wide range of settings in which group theory is applied, including clinics, academia, business, and community. With so much knowledge available, you need a starting point to understand the core concepts, and from there you can follow your interests. To have a background for Directive Group, you might start with the literature on inpatient group therapy approaches. The end of this chapter lists recommended references and resources which are basic and helpful to learning about leading groups.

The best way to begin to understand group processes is to combine a conceptual approach with experiential learning. Courses in group dynamics frequently use this approach by having the class members study their own behavior in the group, sometimes assigning five or so students to select a project and work on it. The important learning from this assignment is reflected in the journal in which the student explores the processes experienced, such as how the task was selected, how decisions were made, how conflicts emerged and were managed, how standards were set, and how the task was completed. Usually the student writes a paper at the end summarizing what was learned and relating the situations experienced to the theories studied.

Only by being in a group specifically designed to study itself can you break down the natural resistance to looking at behavior patterns and actually see the forces that influence the group as a whole. You start to realize the importance of your background and perceptions and the assumptions you make when observing other people. You can see how well your judgment about people holds true from your first impression to the time when you know them fairly intimately. You can see the effects of various styles of communication and patterns of leadership. You can learn what happens when you give feedback or deal with conflict. You can experience the developmental stages of the group, from becoming a member and developing cohesion, to completing the emotional and task components.

Once you have some experience with group processes, other experiences may be of interest. The National Training Laboratories (NTL) Institute, A.K. Rice Institute, and University Associates are three national private organizations that sponsor conferences on group dynamics. NTL is famous for the sensitivity training groups it led in the sixties. Now the organization has a week-long human interaction training lab which is central to their program and is a prerequisite for most of their other offerings. The purpose of the lab is to gain insight into everyday communication and the effect your behavior has on others. A group such as this is an excellent way to learn group dynamics. Although these dynamics may not be immediately applicable to Directive Group, they are important for improving staff relations, leading groups which deal with healthier individuals, and for understanding how Directive Group uses these dynamics in alternate ways.

The A.K. Rice Institute offers weekend and week-long conferences which involve studying the authority relations in the group. Using theory based on systems thinking and unconscious processes, participants can apply the experience primarily to group behavior in organizations. Issues concerning sexism, racism, empowerment, and competency frequently emerge that are largely impossible to work through in an ordinary work environment, but are nevertheless present. This type of group experience is most applicable to the leader's personal development and to political dealings in the health care setting.

There are also workshops specially designed to develop group-related skills. University Associates often offers programs on Training the Trainer, Developing Leadership Abilities, and Learning to Negotiate. The reason I bring these opportunities to your attention is to emphasize the point that there is a lot to learn about leading groups. Through participating in groups, you realize the responsibility of all of the members in making the group successful. You, as the leader, can't do it all, even if you want to.

Therefore, just because we have all been in groups our whole lives — in the family, at school, and in recreation — it doesn't mean we understand what makes a group a group, why one group is different from another, and what to do if the group isn't working. At a minimum, even if you don't participate in extra experiential group conferences, try the types of groups and activities you structure for patients on yourself. Do a practice group with fellow students or staff members. It is very illuminating to see what it feels like to have to deal with your own fears of failure, feelings of competition, experience of boredom, or consequences of absences or lateness. You may not realize how bossy you sound or how your lack of direction causes the group to fragment until you experience others doing the same thing to you.

Once you get a sense of how you behave in groups and are sensitive to observing the processes which occur in groups, you can form a perspective on the factors that encourage effective group work and those that do not. You can start to focus on the wide range of therapy groups and the different ways the process can be perceived and applied therapeutically. You can realize which norms are unique to your setting and which are common to most groups. You will also know when you are dealing with the end of the continuum of behaviors which constitute extreme emotional disturbance and when you are in a more adaptive range.

Comparing Groups in Inpatient and Outpatient Settings

In order to lead treatment groups effectively, you need to understand the individuals for whom the groups are designed. Short-term inpatient groups with very disturbed adults are different from outpatient groups with more stable individuals (Table 1-1). Primarily, people are hospitalized because of an inability to function. Groups in the inpatient setting are affected by this fact in ways that outpatient groups are not, even though the outpatients may have long-standing emotional disturbances and be in as great a need for treatment as the inpatients.

One obvious difference between the two settings is the open nature of inpatient groups. There is no time when the group officially begins and the members agree to meet for twelve sessions, as they might in a group in which there can be more control over scheduling. Because of the constant influx of patients, strategies need to be devised which encourage cohesiveness quickly and maintain the culture of the group regardless of who is in it. (Principles of programming groups are addressed in Chapter 11.)

Another major difference is the level of pathology. Because inpatient groups usually have sicker patients, you can't rely on them to have or be able to use effective group member skills. In some cases the inpatient group is designed to teach group interaction skills, such as a task group. In other situations the group has to be designed to compensate for the lack of skill, such as the Directive Group.

	Inpatient Groups	*Outpatient Groups*
Nature of Group	Open -- constant influx of new referrals to and discharges from group	Usually closed -- individuals selected for specific group and continue until group terminates
Level of Pathology	Acute, severe dysfuction -- behavior usually changes quickly	Behavior is fairly stable -- underlying problems addressed
Setting's Effect on Contact	Institutionalized -- patients and staff have extended contact beyond group sessions	Clinic or community -- patients and staff generally only meet during group sessions
Mix of Individuals	Heterogeneous in terms of age and diagnosis and sometimes levels of function	More homogeneous groups of individuals by age, diagnosis, and ego strength
Cohesiveness	Low degree of cohesiveness -- culture created by leaders and carried on through experienced members	Moderate to high degree of cohesiveness -- trust developed through stages over time

Table 1-1. Differences Between Inpatient and Outpatient Groups.

A third fundamental difference is that inpatient groups take place in an institutional setting where patients live and staff work for an extended period of time. This situation causes group dynamics which frequently pervade the whole ward. For example, suicide attempts, violent patients, and quiet rooms occupied with very disturbed individuals all cause emotional havoc. Fluctuations also result from the anticipation of and recuperation from weekends and holidays, when there are more visitors, fewer staff, and less group structure.

The mix of patients at any one time can also affect the tenor of the ward. A patient in a manic state, several energetic adolescents, a subgroup of drug abusers, more organically impaired elderly patients, or the readmission of chronic schizophrenic patients can tax the ward in different ways. Staff may need to be more vigilant, and resentment builds in the nursing staff when they get pulled from valued meetings to individually monitor the most disturbed patients. Sometimes there is a sense of failure with revolving door patients and frustration with patients who seem to be inappropriate admissions, not the types of patients the unit perceives that it treats best.

Sometimes in inpatient groups there are staff dynamics which get played out due to feelings about a "special" patient; for instance, a physician or a "rich and famous" individual, or a special relationship between a staff member and his or her assigned patient, which the team perceives as too permissive or punitive. The unit is also very affected by major staff turnovers, even those off the ward, such as the hiring of a new director for the department of psychiatry.

All of these situations carry with them palpable tensions. To the extent they can be understood, behavior is not acted out but is discussed and becomes meaningful. When underlying dynamics are not discovered, behavior frequently gets unpredictable. For example, patients may not attend groups as regularly, there may be more attempts by patients to leave the unit without medical advice (AMAs and AWOLs), and staff may resort to more rigid, less individualized treatment plans.

As a small-group leader, understanding the ward issues will help you to plan compatible activities and to predict likely group responses. As a staff member, you have a responsibility to make sense of the processes as they appear to you and to work to support healthy ward functioning. As an individual, understanding group dynamics helps you not feel unrealistically responsible for solving every patient problem and allows you to leave your work at work, where it belongs.

Developing Self-Awareness

Self-awareness helps you to evaluate your values and skills. Do you believe in the kind of groups you are leading? Do you think the approach makes sense for the types of problems you are trying to address? Is the group structure and content respectful of the patients' needs? Do you have the training required to lead the group effectively? Are there special skills you need to acquire? Are you better off using a co-leader to balance out style or roles?

Being sensitive to patient needs begins with being aware of your own. Working on a short-term inpatient psychiatric unit means you need to learn the psychiatric diagnoses for a wide range of patients. You need to know the developmental issues common to adolescents, adults, and elderly individuals. You need a way to understand the different meanings the same behavior may have and how to appreciate the complexities of human nature. Here is another place, as with learning group therapy, where theory is essential. For instance, psychoanalytic theory helps explain defenses and how they work to protect individuals under usual conditions, and how they break down under stress, especially a stress such as an acute psychotic episode. In fact, some psychiatrists view psychosis as a defense against extreme anxiety. The key to using all this knowledge effectively is to become personally involved with it and apply what fits to yourself and your relationships.

Remember the stories about medical students thinking they have every disease they study? Well, trying on pathology is not a bad idea. As you study mental disorders, you can easily distance yourself from the material and say to yourself "not me." You familiarize yourself with the Diagnostic and Statistical Manual (DSM III-R)[2] criteria for diagnoses, learn which medications are appropriate for which symptoms, and eventually think through how each disorder affects everyday functioning. If you don't relate the symptoms to your own experience, there is a danger of treating patients as objects.

Almost all mental diseases are extremes of ordinary everyday behavior. For instance, everyone has to eat each day and make conscious or unconscious decisions about how much, what type of food, and how often to eat. That does not cause everyone to have anorexia nervosa or bulimia. But if you try to imagine under what conditions you could become obsessed with food, using it for control battles or perfectionistic strivings, you will have more empathy for people who suffer with these conditions.

In Directive Group most of the patients have an extreme dysfunction of thoughts, feelings, and behavior. Your being able to relate to them in a caring and genuine way is very important. While you probably never have been psychotic or experienced hallucinations, can you imagine the terror of having dreams while you are awake? Think about patients with clinical depression. You may wonder how they can let their appearance go. Yet, on a smaller scale, if you ever spent a few all-nighters on a project, what happened to washing your hair, changing clothes, and keeping your room neat? Hardly anyone has been spared the pain of a close relationship dissolving, a family member dying, or the loss of a valuable personal object. Our experiences of loss and grieving can help us relate to those with an extended and severe depression.

Similarly, think about your reaction to a patient with alcoholism who is still denying the illness. Do you feel empathic towards him or her and the resistance to accept such a blow to the self? Or do you feel impatient and irritable? How about a feisty young adult with a diagnosis of borderline personality disorder? Do you think the person should be able to control the insatiable demands and his or her erratic behavior? Are you more tolerant of the lack of control a person exhibits who has paranoid ideation?

It is not that you should expect yourself to be a saint; no one else is. The issue is finding the humanity within yourself to feel with and for the people for whom you are hired to provide service. The challenge is to explore the nature of a helping relationship not from a position of superiority and martyrdom, but from a view of understanding and collaboration.

Getting Started

Now that we have looked at some of the generic areas group leaders need to know, we are ready to focus on Directive Group. If you don't have a background in group dynamics, you may want to take a course or get some apprentice level group experience first. Similarly, if you have a limited understanding of psychopathology and the demands of an inpatient setting, you may want to familiarize yourself more with these areas. Students may be using this book as part of a course in which they can practice leading activities and setting goals for minimally functioning individuals. Fieldwork students will be developing these competencies as well as their self-awareness at the same time they may be apprenticing as Directive Group co-leaders.

Experienced mental health practitioners who want to learn to use Directive Group as a form of group therapy may want to examine your comfortableness with activities, your present theoretical framework for formulating treatment plans, and your educational preparation for this type of group. Those of you who plan to adapt this group to other settings and populations will probably want to become comfortable with how this group is planned and led on the short-term unit. Then you will have a fuller understanding of the rationale for making necessary changes. The same approach is recommended if you are an occupational therapist in a rehabilitation setting and have little recent group experience. You may want to collaborate with an experienced group leader to think through the application ideas and practice co-leadership skills.

Now that you have addressed the content areas for running this group, you need to assess the process by which you learn best. Inventories are available which may help you determine your learning style. Do you learn best by observation, reading and reflection, concrete experiences, or some combination of these? Some people prefer to think things through before trying out their ideas; others learn better by just jumping in. Some like to work alone, while others feel their intellect is engaged when in concert with a partner or team. Even without using an instrument, you can figure out your preferences by analyzing your responses to several situations in which you learned something. Or consider if you were going to learn a new sport or outside interest: how would you choose to go about learning it? When would you need the most encouragement to keep going — when you are getting started, maintaining the pace and practicing, or coming to closure? What I am encouraging you to do is think about your learning style and approach learning about Directive Group in a way that is most comfortable for you.

A third way to approach learning Directive Group is from a developmental perspective in which you consider the sequence of stages people generally go through when learning something new. Certain issues are easier to deal with

Table 1-2. Commitment to Learning and Change

Area of Interest	Typical Questions	Level of Concern	Possible Action Steps and Resources
Getting interested and oriented	What is the group about? What materials are needed? Where do I get more information? Where is the innovation currently being used?	*Informational* The practitioner is concerned about learning more of a general nature about the innovation and what is required to use it. After becoming familiar with it, a decision is made whether or not to use the approach.	Read general descriptions of the group (such as article in *AJOT*, July 1985). Talk to other practitioners about their experiences with this group. View a videotape on the group to see what it is about (See list of References and Resources Chapter 2). Skim this book and read Chapter 2. Review activities in the Appendix. Decide if you want to make a commitment to learning more about the group.
Learning the mechanics of leading Directive Group	What commitments are required? How would my group leadership skills change? What would be expected from other staff members? How much time would be involved?	*Personal* The practitioner is appraising his or her present clinical role and preparing for the ways that role may have to change in order to use the innovation.	Consider your current clinical role and group leadership skills. Examine this book in detail (especially Chapters 3-8). Be knowledgeable about the format of the group, the sequence of events, typical activities, usual group needs, referral criteria, goals, procedures for monitoring progress and documentation, the theoretical framework, and leadership functions. Consider needs of your setting, co-leadership options, scheduling, and patient characteristics.
Gaining clinical experience for leading the group routinely	How do I get materials ready and accessible? Are patients doing what they should be doing? How do I get all the activities ordered and prepared? Why planning is taking so much of my time?	*Managerial* The practitioner is concerned about organization and logistics. There is a need to be able to anticipate beyond day to day problems. Strategies need to be developed to decrease preparation and documentation time.	Practice planning the daily sessions, setting individual patient goals, and using the activities in the Appendix. Divide up co-leadership responsibilities for ordering and organizing supplies, writing notes, and communication with staff about referrals and follow-up. Use time management techniques, set priorities, delegate when possible, and ask for assistance when necessary. Read Chapter 12 to apply self-management concepts.

Adapted from Loucks, S., Hall, G. (Spring 1977). Assessing and facilitating innovations: A new approach. Ed Technol, 18-21.
Adapted from Barris, R., Kaplan, K. (1986). Theories of change. In Robertson, S. (Ed.): Mental Health SCOPE: Strategies, Concepts, and Opportunities for Program Development and Evaluation.

Table 1-2. Commitment to Learning and Change *(continued)*

Area of Interest	Typical Questions	Level of Concern	Possible Action Steps and Resources
Developing flexibility and creativity within the group	Are patients using the group effectively? Are they learning anything meaningful? What changes can be made to make the group even better? Is the group really consistent with the theoretical framework?	*Consequential* The practitioner is primarily concerned with the innovation's impact on patients. Materials and procedures are varied, either for the group as a whole or in reference to individual patients.	Think of new activity ideas for your specific patients, settings, and needs. Observe the group process over time and reflect on your experiences. Review your documentation (patient assessments, progress ratings, and achievement of outcome goals) and compare them to original expectations. Get feedback from co-leaders, patients, and other staff. Focus on making adaptations of goals, theoretical framework, and referral criteria as needed. Re-read Chapters 6, 8, and 9.
Conceptualizing a systems perspective for program development	Is there continuity from this group to the rest of the program? Are other group leaders using these principles in a similar way? Can we start working together and coordinating what we are doing?	*Collaborative* The practitioner is concerned about relating what he or she is doing with the innovation to what others are doing as a way to increase the effect on the patients' total treatment.	Share resources and ideas with other staff. Develop interdisciplinary task forces to collaborate on need for changes and ways to do it. Offer group co-leadership training and supervision to other staff and students. Examine the total group program comparing staff perceptions about its effectiveness. Plan program evaluation, quality assurance, or clinical research studies. Read chapters 9, 10, and 11 and do the exercises provided with other staff.
Working on further innovations	How can I broaden my vision? What can I do to increase professional growth? How can this group help achieve maximum outcomes for psychiatric patients in other settings and for the health care system as a whole?	*Regenerative* The practitioner is concerned about whether other innovations exist and if they would achieve the same goals more effectively.	Combine other approaches with these group principles and apply to other populations, programs, and facilities. Look for other ideas to supplement or replace this innovation (Review lists of References and Resources). Get involved in teaching and consulting in relation to group treatment and program development. Do comparative research studies on this and compatible treatment groups. Read books such as *Occupational Therapy in Mental Health: A Guide to Outcomes Research* to stimulate ideas about increasing treatment and efficacy and developing new approaches to psychosocial evaluation and treatment.

once other material is mastered. The following model may help you realize, and be comfortable with, your own level of energy for learning and help you pace yourself for the future (Table 1-2).

The model is adapted from teacher education literature and a previous application to the process of learning a new theory.[1,3] It is based on principles of adult learners, such as taking responsibility for both what you learn as well as for how to go about gathering and integrating the necessary information. Learning progresses from becoming familiar about something, to gaining knowledge about it, to understanding it in relation to other concepts and ideas, to ultimately applying it to actual situations. The goal of this book is to provide assistance at each level, emphasizing the whys and hows critical to effective implementation.

Using the Directive Group as an example of an innovation, the model suggests that in order to make a change in our professional behavior, we first need to make a commitment. This involves becoming aware of our level of concerns. Specific questions are typical of each phase in the process of implementing an innovation. By realizing what actions we are developing, we can better locate appropriate resources to help us change.

For example, at the first level you are curious about starting the group. You probably are asking questions such as, What is the group about? What materials are needed? Where do I go for more information? Where is the innovation currently being used? These questions are typical of an "informational" level of concern. They suggest various action steps and resources, which can be selected based on your learning style preferences and professional needs, such as reading an article, viewing a videotape, or talking to group leaders.

This approach stresses the point that learning requires a commitment. To the extent the material is of interest and is enjoyable to learn, the process of learning is more likely to be meaningful and efficient. I hope you have that experience learning about Directive Group; that is the experience we try to create for the participants in the group. By actively engaging them, you engage yourself. Fulfillment from leading the group comes from the challenge of continuously responding to patients changing functional needs, and responding to your own needs for personal development and professional satisfaction. It is this mutually enhancing quality which, for me, is the essence of Directive Group.

References

1. Barris, R., Kaplan, K. (1986). Theories of change. In Robertson, S. (Ed.): Mental Health SCOPE: Strategies, Concepts, and Opportunities for Program Developmental Evaluation. Rockville, MD: The American Occupational Therapy Association, pp. 85-90.
2. DSM-IIIR: Diagnostic and Statistical Manual of Mental Disorders, 3rd ed. revised. (1987). Washington, DC: American Psychiatric Association.
3. Loucks, S., Hall, G. (Spring, 1977). Assessing and facilitating innovations: A new approach. Educ Technol, 18-21. Vol. 17, 2.

Suggested Readings and Resources

Group Dynamics

Bion, W. (1961). Experiences in Groups and Other Papers. New York: Basic Books.

Cartwright, D & Zander, A (1968). Group Dynamics : Research Theory (3rd ed). New York: Harper & Row.

Corey, G, Corey, M, Callanan, P & Russell, J (1982). Group Technique. Monterey, California: Brooks/Cole.

Johnson, D & Johnson, F (1982). Joining Together: Group Therapy and Group Skills. Englewood Cliffs, NJ: Prentice-Hall.

Luft, J (1984). Group Processes: An Introduction to Group Dynamics. Palo Alto, CA: Mayfield.

Napier, R & Gershenfeld M (1981). Groups: Theory and Experience (2nd ed). Boston: Houghton Mifflin.

Sampson, E & Marthas, M (1981). Group Process for the Health Professions. New York: John Wiley & Sons.

Yalom, I. (1983). Inpatient Group Psychotherapy. New York: Basic Books.

Yalom, I (1975). The Theory and Practice of Group Psychotherapy (2nd ed). New York: Basic Books.

Group Experience

AK Rice Institute. PO Box 39102, Washington, DC 20016. (202) 857-8447.

NTL Institute. PO Box 9155, Rosslyn Station/Arlington, Virginia 22209. (703) 527-1500.

University Associates. 8517 Production Avenue, San Diego, California 92121. (619) 578-5900.

Self Assessment

Keegan, W (1982). Keegan Type Indicator. Warren Keegan Associates Press, 10 Halsted Place, Rye, New York 10580.

Kolb, D, Rubin, I & McIntyre, J (1971). The learning style inventory. Organizational Psychology: An Experimental Approach. Englewood Cliffs, New Jersey: Prentice Hall.

Purtillo, R (1971). Health Professional/Patient Interaction. Philadelphia: W.B. Saunders.

Rezler, A (1974). Learning Preference Inventory. University of Illinois, at the Medical Center, CED, 806 South Wood Street, Chicago, Illinois 60612.

Scott, D (1980). How to Put More Time in Your Life. New York: Signet.

Short Term Treatment

Bradlee, L (1984). The use of groups in short-term psychiatric settings. Occupational Therapy in Mental Health, 4(3), 47-57.

Kibel, H (1981). A conceptual model for short-term inpatient group psychotherapy. American Journal of Psychiatry, 138, 74-80.

Klein, R (1977). Inpatient group psychotherapy: Practical considerations and special problems. International Journal of Group Psychotherapy, 27, 201-214.

Klein, R & Kugel, B (1981). Inpatient group psychotherapy from a system perspective: Reflections through a glass darkly. International Journal of Group Psychotherapy, 31, 311-328.

Maves, P. & Schulz, J. (1985). Inpatient group treatment on short-term acute care units. Hospital & Community Psychiatry, 36, 69-72.

Teaching Learning

Harvey, J (1979). Learning not to teach. Exchange: The Organizational Behavior Teaching Journal, 4(3), 19-21.

Knowles, M (1975). Self Directed Learning. New York: Association Press.

Knowles, M (1986). Using Learning Contracts. San Francisco: Jossey-Bass.

Lawrence, G (1982). People Types and Tiger Stripes: A Practical Guide to Learning Styles. Gainesville, Florida: Center for Applications of Psychological Type.

CHAPTER 2

THEY CAN DO IT!

Describing Directive Group

Before we can explore the process of leading groups, we need a common starting point. This chapter describes Directive Group and touches on issues that will be elaborated in later chapters. "They can do it!" refers to the belief that even patients who are extremely disorganized and disturbed can be actively helped to change. Why wait for them to reorganize when you can have a positive affect on their recovery? Medications are not enough. Psychosocial dysfunctions require psychosocial interventions. If your unit is like the one I worked on, about one-third of the patients fit the description of minimally functioning adults. Even though they are a diverse crew, in the right environment they form a workable group in which exciting things can happen.

Where We Were: A Traditional Program

Directive Group was designed over ten years ago for a 34-bed inpatient unit *(6 North) of a university hospital in a large metropolitan area. At that time, the staff consisted of attending psychiatrists and residents, nurses and psychiatric technicians, social workers, a psychologist, an art therapist, an occupational therapist, and a therapeutic recreation specialist. The program offered group psychotherapy and art therapy in heterogeneous groupings of patients by teams. The recreation therapy and ward meetings were generally open to all patients, while the occupational therapy groups were organized by levels of functioning. A few of the staff, including myself, kept noticing that a cluster of patients didn't seem to benefit from the treatment program or fit into these groups. These were the extremely disturbed patients — on medications, in quiet rooms, and on one-to-one nursing contacts.

How did we know these patients weren't benefiting from, weren't ready for, or couldn't tolerate verbal group therapy? We saw that they could hardly sit still for five minutes at a time and attend to conversation. They were so focused on their own thoughts and feelings that they weren't responsive to the thoughts and feelings of others. They often interrupted or disrupted the group process. It appeared that these behaviors occurred not because the patients meant to be annoying, but because they didn't have the skills required to function in this verbal arena for 45 minutes.

We tried to think about what to do. The observations about these patients was in the context of considering other complaints about the program. On the one hand, we knew we had a basically solid program, good staff, a supportive director, and an adequate budget. We had learned to be flexible about sharing space and supplies. On the other hand, we wanted to decrease fragmentation and improve the quality of treatment offered. We knew we could have a really great program if we pulled together as a staff and built on our strengths.

Where We Went: A Coordinated System of Group Therapy

We brainstormed and came up with a three-tiered group therapy program. The middle level psychotherapy group became the "supportive" group, the highest level group psychotherapy was called "interpretive," and the lowest level group was the "directive" group. Over time the highest group merged with supportive and Directive Group came into its own. Other groups were offered based on patient needs and levels of functioning. The occupational therapy department expanded and became responsible for supervising related services, such as therapeutic recreation and various activity-oriented student programs.

Currently, the unit offers a continuum of services, including day treatment and outpatient programs. Adolescent, adult, and elderly patients are admitted for evaluation and treatment of acute emotional problems. During an average two- or three-week stay, patients participate in a wide range of therapeutic services typical of short-term programs: individual psychotherapy, primary nursing care, psychotropic medications, family therapy, occupational therapy, therapeutic recreation, and group therapy. Typical groups offered include Supportive Group (verbal group therapy), Task Group, Assertiveness Training, Exercise Group, Activity Planning, Leisure Awareness, and Community Meeting. A more in-depth discussion of program development is presented in Chapters 9-11. In this chapter I want to focus on the most innovative change, Directive Group, and share with you part of our experiences.

Verbal Group Psychotherapy

The cornerstone of many group treatment programs on inpatient units is verbal group psychotherapy. This modality is accorded high status because of two factors: most often the psychiatrists or residents in training lead this group, and in terms of the medical model hierarchy, they are on top; and there is a long history of using group therapy effectively with psychiatric patients.

However, there are two problems with this emphasis. The first is that traditional group therapy methods are not adapted for the special needs of short-term units. New approaches are needed to address the constant influx of patients, the wide range of ages and diagnoses represented in the patient population, the problems of reimbursement, and the two-to three-week average length of stay. The second problem is organizational. Most inpatient units have interdisciplinary staff who work as teams. There may be nurses, social workers, psychologists, occupational therapists, and a variety of activity-oriented therapists. Teams are a form of horizontal organizational structure designed to support each person's contribution to assessment and treatment planning.

Most inpatient units also rely on a hierarchical organization, which supports ultimate accountability and clear delineation of roles and responsibilities. However, the hierarchical organization often is viewed as a symbol of staff inequality — the pecking order notion. This runs counter to the way the horizontal organization is seen, as reinforcing each professional's work as different, but equally valuable. The challenge for the ward is to learn to deal with the tensions created by using these two organizational models simultaneously. For example, we elevated the value of the nonmedical professionals through the process of revising our whole group program. By viewing it as a comprehensive system, we established ways to coordinate diverse interests. The program then required the interconnection of multiple inputs to be effective.

An Alternative: Directive Group Therapy

Irvin Yalom, a guru of group psychotherapy known for his seminal text, *The Theory and Practice of Group Psychotherapy*,[6] greatly helped clinicians understand the changes needed in the traditional approaches by writing the book *Inpatient Group Psychotherapy*.[7] He discussed the heterogeneity of inpatient units and formulated principles designed to address the current needs through *two* levels of groups. The higher level group stressed focusing on problems through agendas, giving lots of support, and using here-and-now interactions. The lower level group, the Focus Group, he modeled after the Directive Group. Yalom tailored the basic ideas to his own setting, patient needs, and leadership style.

As is appropriate, and to be expected if you use Directive Group as the seed from which to develop your own program, there are some differences between the two groups. The important point is that the development of a lower level psychotherapy group underscores the fundamental value of the Directive Group — that psychotic and other extremely disturbed adults have real and special needs which must be addressed in groups specifically designed to meet their needs and level of functioning. The patients need a therapeutic environment which builds on what is there and does not make them uncomfortably aware of what is lacking.

Theoretical Framework

Before describing Directive Group, I want to talk about the theoretical framework because it will provide a context for thinking about the components of the group. Initially, I developed the group using other criteria, then I learned the model of human occupation and redefined the group within that framework. The group was originally based on a developmental framework in which patient problems were defined across multiple categories, such as cognitive, perceptual, social, and psychological capacities. All of the patients on the unit were assessed according to these categories and divided into one of three levels of functioning. This approach was compatible with the director of the unit's functional orientation and became the basis for reorganizing the entire group program.

During my masters degree program, I studied the model of human occupation[3] intensely. I was attracted to the theory's grounding in systems thinking, which helped me explain the similar patterns I had observed in how individual patients, treatment groups, and the unit as a whole functioned and changed. I also was impressed with the way in which the theory enlarged on my understanding of the features that made Directive Group effective. I ended up using the model of human occupation to reconceptualize the Directive Group and the organization of the comprehensive group treatment program. I found the model of human occupation useful because it embraces interdisciplinary views and emphasizes concepts important for psychiatric patients, such as adaptive behavior, roles, change through action, environmental interaction, and intrinsic motivation. The model's focus on occupational behavior is consistent with the short-term unit's goals of improving patients functioning and enabling them to return to the community. The model allows for integrating information from different professionals pertaining to such factors as the patient's environment and support system. The model also enables the occupational therapist to specify an organized approach to the assessment and treatment process while delineating the scope of services.

Not everyone on our unit shared my theoretical bent. Yet, the program continued to function in a coordinated fashion and the Directive Group continued to operate effectively. I think this is because the model of human occupation is consistent with solid clinical practice. Staff may differ on the reasons why they think people get sick, react to stress, or make changes in their lives. They may have alternative explanations for the type of interventions best used in a group. But to have a dynamic and proactive program, staff need to think abstractly about their daily work. Without a theoretical framework, the clinician lacks a coherent way to organize knowledge, ascribe meaning to observations, or predict outcomes. I bring this up to both reinforce the importance of using a theoretical framework and to acknowledge that leading the Directive Group does not require commitment to the model of human occupation. To me, it has the greatest explanatory power. It also has the potential to be used flexibly.

Because the Directive Group was developed using a more empirical approach, many of the phrases used on the referral form and rating scale are not written in the strict language of the model or in the order that they are usually presented. The behavioral descriptions are linked with model components; but if the group had been designed initially with the model of human occupation as the organizing framework, the phrasing would have reflected this more strongly. This point is also important from a practical aspect. Clinical settings exert influences in the design of treatment strategies. Strict adherence to theoretical constructs may not be as easy to attain in practice as it is in the classroom or research lab. Compromises in the speed in which changes can be accepted by patients and staff are often necessary. (Chapters 10 and 11 treat the issues of change and program development more fully.) The issue for you is to see the bridges between theory and practice as described in this manual. Although you may choose to articulate a different one or to use this one differently, you should use a theoretical approach with the Directive Group.

One of the realities of describing clinical practice is that it is hard to write about something that is constantly evolving. Even though Directive Group has stood the test of time, there are still areas which can be improved and developed. What I try to do in this manual is give you the best of what we found to work during the six years I co-led the group and to explain the rationale sufficiently so that you can evaluate the similarities with your own setting, needs, and preferences. Then, with this manual as a resource, you can make the adjustments necessary, given your own constraints and circumstances.

Basic Concepts from the Model of Human Occupation

Many resources exist describing the model of human occupation. I will provide only a brief introduction to the concepts here. The model of human occupation applies systems theory concepts to the occupational behavior of humans. Occupational behavior refers to the work, play, and self-maintenance activities with which individuals are occupied each day. General systems theory is applicable to all phenomena, from organizations, families, small groups, and individuals to cells. A hierarchy of knowledge organizes phenomena by levels of complexity.

Occupational therapy knowledge spans many levels, from motor development to cultural meanings. When an individual has a disease, trauma, or developmental disability, the whole system is affected — body, mind, daily routine, pattern of achievement, and relation to social groups. The occupational therapy process involves mobilizing an individual's capacities through occupation to retain quality of life. The organizing effects of occupation extend the spectrum from maladaptive to adaptive functioning.

Human occupation is conceptualized at the level of open systems. This means individuals are constantly in interaction with the physical and social environment, and they maintain and change their behavior through a cycle of intake, throughput, output, and feedback. Occupational behavior or actions are the output of the human system. Feedback provides information on the consequences of actions, allowing for the intake of information. Throughput is the means by which a person integrates this information and continues the open system cycle. According to the model, the throughput of an individual is composed of three subsystems organized into a hierarchy: volition, habituation, and performance. The volition subsystem has to do with the individual's capacity to make choices, which is in turn a reflection of feeling effective (personal causation), experiencing pleasure (interests), and knowing what is personally important (values). The habituation subsystem involves making actions a part of a daily routine through the development of habits and roles. The performance subsystem enables an individual to produce action skillfully through the ability to think clearly (process skills), move with agility (motor skills), and interact with others comfortably (communication/interaction skills) (Figure 2-1).

Treatment is guided by principles of systems theory based on rules of hierarchy. One rule is that the higher levels guide the lower levels. This means therapy should focus on the higher level, in this case, the volitional subsystem. For example, a patient's interests, goals, and self-confidence should guide the group leader's selection of occupations and activities. A second rule states that the lower levels constrain the higher levels. This means therapy should be organized at the lowest level, in most cases, the performance subsystem. If an individual, for instance, can't concentrate on simple tasks or communicate effectively, then therapy should start by developing those basic skills.

A third rule is that any dysfunction affects all the levels. Therefore, therapy should address all the levels (skills, habits, and roles) and use the higher levels to compensate for permanent disorganization imposed by lower levels. For example, some patients, after extended drug abuse, need to change jobs (representing the higher level) to find one more compatible with reduced cognitive abilities (the lower level).

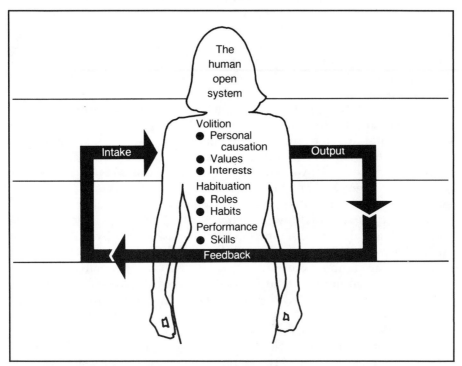

Figure 2-1. The open system representing human occupation.
From Kielhofner, G. (Ed.). (1985). A Model of Human Occupation: Theory and Application. Baltimore: Williams & Wilkins, p. 35.

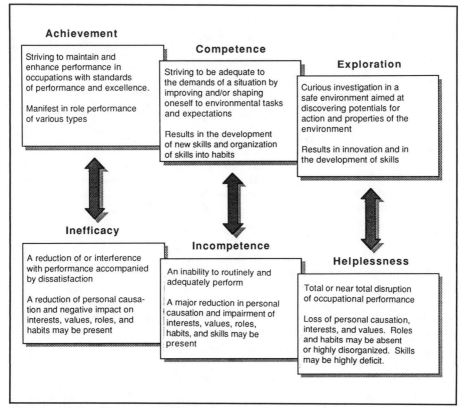

Table 2-1. Levels of Function and Dysfunction.
Adapted from Kielhofner, G. (Ed.). (1985). A Model of Human Occupation: Theory and Application. Baltimore: Williams & Wilkins, pp. 65, 70.

Using the Model of Human Occupation for Program Development

Specifically, I used the model in three main ways to redefine the program. First, the model provides a way to conceptualize group treatment as the creation of a therapeutic environment in which patients interact to learn about themselves and enact changes. The environment is created by providing necessary levels of arousal, enhancing internal control, stimulating interest and meaning in activities, and conveying expectations relevant to patient needs, goals, and roles. Every group in a program, then, can be examined for the specific ways the therapeutic environment is created.

Second, the model specifies a continuum of functional and dysfunctional occupational behavior represented by six levels. Degrees of adaptive behavior range from exploration to competence and achievement. These correspond with three maladaptive patterns from helplessness to incompetence and inefficacy (Table 2-1). Because we were working to overcome levels of dysfunction by supporting function, we organized our groups by the three functional levels (Table 2-2) Criteria for each level were further developed and used to organize each group in the total program (see Chapter 11).

Exploration level groups are organized at the simplest level of challenge to

**Achievement
Level Groups**

Designed to help patients integrate skills into daily life roles.
Patients are active in identifying
their learning needs relative to
work, leisure, and interpersonal
relationships.

**Competence
Level Groups**

Designed to help patients
expand skills and identify goals,
interests, and needs. Therapists
involve patients in collaborative
decision making and cooperative
interaction.

**Exploratory
Level Groups**

Designed to help patients
develop basic skills in a nonthreatening, structured setting.
Therapists are largely responsible
for selection of activities and
organization of the treatment
environment.

Examples:
Assertiveness training

Community meeting

Leisure awareness

Examples:
Supportive group

Task group

Activity planning

Evening activities

Examples:
Exercise group

School program

Directive group

Table 2-2. Hierarchical Structure of Group Treatment Program.

help the most disorganized patients develop basic skills. Competence level
groups are appropriate for patients who have basic skills but may need to
integrate them into habit patterns. These groups are designed to help
patients expand their skills and identify goals, interests, and needs for
meaning and action. As patients approach discharge, they begin to learn new
ways to cope with problems experienced at home and in the community.
Groups at the achievement level are designed to help patients integrate skills
into their daily life roles.

Third, the model serves to identify the variables necessary for assessing
patient behavior and specifying treatment goals. Referral criteria can be
developed based on behavioral descriptions of the most typical patient problems addressed in each group and translated into the language of the model
for consistency (see Chapter 5). Going from the structure of the whole
treatment program to the general aspects of each group, we can now focus in
on Directive Group specifically.

What Is Directive Group?

Directive Group is a special form of group treatment designed to meet the
needs of acutely ill, minimally functioning patients. These patients represent
a wide range of diagnoses, ages, and problems (which will be elaborated
later), but all have extreme difficulty taking care of themselves, even with
supervision. They are unable to function in almost all areas and have serious
impairment of communication and judgment capacities.

When people first hear the term "directive" they think it must mean telling
patients what to do, that is, being very directive. The term directive refers to
the active and supportive way in which the group leaders structure the
environment to assure maximum participation of all members. The group
prepares extremely disturbed patients in a short-term setting for the most

commonly available forms of group psychotherapy and activity-oriented groups. The purpose of the group is to assist patients in reorganizing their behavior to a basic level of competence. Most group programs begin at this level because these patients can generally take care of basic self-care activities and get themselves to group. They can also stay in the group for 45 minutes without being overly disruptive. Once in the group, patients at a basic level of competence can:

-Globally grasp the purpose of the group

-Follow simple instructions

-Tolerate interaction with others

-Maintain at least a simple degree of conversation

-Concentrate on a task or topic enough to participate.

In occupational therapy literature these are the groups recently described by Howe and Schwartzberg as the functional model.[2] Similar to the Directive Group in aim, they assist an individual's adaptation through purposeful, self-initiated, spontaneous, and group-centered activity. The main difference between the functional group approach and the Directive Group is the level of functioning addressed. Because Directive Group patients are minimally functioning, a range of adaptations are necessary in order to lead the group effectively. Once at a basic level of competence, the functional model is descriptive of a wide variety of groups such as those organized around a theme, specific media, developmental issue, or skill. For patients needing Directive Group, functional group approaches pick up where Directive Group leaves off.

Alternative group models have been developed for low level functioning patients; however, they are primarily designed to meet the needs of the chronically ill in a long-term setting. For instance, Ross[5] describes a five-stage model which has a similar sequence of events as is used in Directive Group. Allen[1] describes another way to organize groups for such patients around their cognitive levels, while King[4] describes a sensory-integrative approach. The nature of these groups and the theoretical frameworks differ from each other and from Directive Group.

What Are the Consequences of Not Having a Directive Group?

In most inpatient settings these patients receive medication, supervision and structure, and individual contact, but no group treatment. Staff assume an attitude of waiting until these patients recompensate before treating them. The problem with this approach is that the patients miss out on an opportunity to be engaged with a constructive, supportive, and corrective experience. They have overwhelming needs, and only a group setting can offer the necessary stimulation for evoking the use of basic skills. Only through a group can the leaders become role models for action, providers of much needed support, and facilitators of collaborative interaction.

Some facilities do offer groups, but they are not specially designed for this population. The patients receive inappropriate treatment which neither helps them nor the other patients in the group. Before Directive Group was instituted in our setting, all the patients attended verbal group therapy three times a week. What happened was that the more organized patients who were benefiting from the discussion got angry and told the disruptive patients to be quiet or eventually asked them to leave. Meanwhile, the patients who were silently hallucinating during the session were ignored because at least the rest of the group could get some work done with them there. At best, the Directive Group types of patients got negative feedback from others and, more usually, did not get their needs met. No one was able to make full use of the group therapy experience in this situation.

Are We Sure Directive Group Works?

Yes and no. First the no. Only carefully controlled research could answer questions such as, Is Directive Group more effective than no group treatment? What is the relative contribution of medication, supervision and structure, and Directive Group on speed and extent of patient recovery? How effective is Directive Group compared with alternative forms of treatment? Here you may reasonably compare Directive Group with verbal group therapy, a parallel craft group, an exercise group, and a structured social skills group.

Have we done this research? No. In our setting we did not have the controls or support available to conduct such studies. Should research be done? Yes, it would be extremely valuable. Is it worthwhile to write extensively about this group without this type of data available? I think so, because I think each professional contributes what he or she can do best, building on the work of those who went before and offering a stepping stone for those who come after. Directive Group has been around for ten years now and most of the bugs are worked out of it. This means others can take this conceptualization of the group and put their energy into researching it, as well as other forms of treatment.

Now the yes. We used to have problems with this subgroup of patients on the unit not benefiting from the groups that were available. Now with an individualized approach to patient care and a group specially designed for this population, that is no longer the case. We tried many approaches in the course of developing Directive Group. We observed Directive Group to be more effective than a parallel craft group because more interaction and active participation is facilitated; more effective than an exercise group because broader individual goals are worked on; and more effective than a social skills group because problems of extreme passivity, confusion, and limited frustration tolerance could be better addressed. These other groups certainly have a place and complement the work of Directive Group. But, for our purpose of meeting the diverse needs of this population, Directive Group works best for developing basic skills and self-direction.

My impression is that most of the patients in Directive Group recompensate faster than they would without the group. Patients generally function more effectively in Directive Group than they do when not in the group, sitting in the lobby or otherwise involved in the ward environment. Their behavior and own report on how they feel improves from the beginning of the group to the end of the session. Thus, my clinical judgment tells me the group serves to elicit more organized behavior and to help maintain more adaptive functioning.

What Are the Main Components of Directive Group?

When starting any group certain factors need to be addressed based on the assessed needs of particular patients in the treatment setting. These factors serve as an outline for designing and describing specific forms of group therapy in which Directive Group is an example. These include: the structure and format of the group, the membership criteria, the context of climate, the leadership roles, the goals, the activities, and the documentation procedures.

Format. The group meets five days a week at a routine time and place. It meets for 45 minutes with a predictable sequence of events: orientation, introduction, warm-up activities, selected activities, and wrap-up. We met from 9:30 to 10:15 a.m. This frequency and duration evolved after trying other options which were not as compatible in our setting. The sessions begin and end promptly to emphasize realistic use of and attention to time. The format is designed to counteract patient problems with disorientation, confusion, and fearfulness. Most patients attend for at least one week.

Membership Criteria. Patients are screened for the group based on behavioral observation. Referral criteria assist staff in identifying patients appropriate for the group. The patients are told they are expected to attend consistently. Nursing staff assist disorganized patients attend on time to ensure continuity of treatment.

Size of the Group. The group can accommodate a wide range of patients, making it responsive to fluctuations in the ward population. The most comfortable size of the group is from 6 to 10 patients with 2 co-leaders, although the group has been run with as few as 2 patients and as many as 15. Clearly, more adaptations are required when the size is at the extremes.

Theoretical Framework. The Directive Group is based on the model of human occupation. This theory helps to conceptualize the level of functioning of the patients and the rationale for many of the therapeutic processes.

Context. The relationship and activites of the group occur in a playful arena, a safe environment, which encourages risk-taking in patients who are threatened by the possibility of failure. The group is organized at the simplest level of challenge to encourage the development of basic skills. This helps patients move from passivity and internal preoccupation to goal-directed processes in which spontaneity and interest in the environment begin to emerge.

Leadership. Co-leaders are necessary to provide role models for action, support, and collaborative interaction. They offer legitimate choices to patients; problems of resistance and lack of motivation are turned into more active and cooperative behavior. The leaders structure the physical environment to reinforce the expectations for performance. They also adapt activities on the spot to meet the changing needs of the group for novelty, complexity, and uncertainty.

Goals. In Directive Group there are four group goals and ten compatible individual patient goals. The group goals encourage cohesiveness, while the individual patient goals allow for increased flexibility for deriving meaning from the group and relating the group experience to the total treatment plan. The group goals include emphasis on increasing participation, interaction, attention, and initiation. An example of an individual goal is to follow instructions on tasks.

Activities. The occupations include a large array of games, crafts, movement activities, and structured communication exercises adapted to the basic level of skills of the patients. They are designed to provide an optimal match between patients' needs for developing cognitive, motor, and interaction skills and the demands of the environment for eliciting such behavior.

Documentation. Patient behavior is evaluated after each group on a four-item rating scale which relates the group goals to outcome criteria. Progress on individual goals are written in the patient chart in the problem-oriented format each week, or more frequently as needed. Patients are discharged from the group when they meet the goals as indicated on the rating scale.

Once you are familiar with Directive Group, you will see how to adapt it for your own purposes. But no matter how you may end up changing the specific goals, activities, referral criteria, or theoretical framework, the following principles embody the essence of Directive Group and should be maintained:

-Provide a predictable routine for patients through the organization of the group and sequence of events (see Chapter 4).

-Establish a baseline of individual patient behavior, monitor daily progress, and document achievement of group goals (see Chapter 5).

-Develop realistic and individualized short-term goals for each patient (see Chapter 6).

-Offer leadership and role models to patients for action, support, and collaborative interaction (see Chapter 7).

-Create a playful arena which legitimizes the activities and interactions of the group and allows patients to develop skills and confidence (see Chapter 7).

-Modify the physical environment and materials to foster patient participation and encourage spontaneity (see Chapter 8).

References

1. Allen, C. (1985). Occupational Therapy for Psychiatric Diseases: Measurement and Management of Cognitive Disabilities. Boston: Little, Brown & Co.

2. Howe, M., Schwartzberg, S. (1986). A Functional Approach to Group Work in Occupational Therapy. Philadelphia: J.B. Lippincott.
3. Kielhofner, G. (Ed.). (1985). A Model of Human Occupation: Theory and Application. Baltimore: Williams & Wilkins.
4. King, L. (1974). A sensory integrative approach to schizophrenia. Am J Occup Ther 28:529-536.
5. Ross, M. (1987). Group Process: Using Therapeutic Activities in Chronic Care. Thorofare, NJ: Charles B. Slack.
6. Yalom, I. (1975). The Theory and Practice of Group Psychotherapy, 2nd ed. New York: Basic Books.
7. Yalom, I. (1983). Inpatient Group Psychotherapy. New York: Basic Books.

Suggested Readings

Directive Group Therapy

Kaplan, K. (Producer). (1982). Directive Group: Treatment for Acute Care Psychiatric Patients (videotape). Washington, DC: The George Washington University Medical Center, Department of Psychiatry.

Kaplan, K. (Producer). (1983). Inpatient Group Treatment: A System for Short-term Psychiatric Programming (videotape). Washington, DC: The George Washington University Medical Center, Department of Psychiatry.

Kaplan, K. (1986). The directive group: Short-term treatment for psychiatric patients with a minimal level of functioning. Am J Occup Ther 40(7):474-481.

Yalom, I. (1983). The lower level psychotherapy group: A working model. In Inpatient Group Psychotherapy. New York: Basic Books, pp. 275-312.

General Systems Theory

Boulding, K. (1956). General systems theory — The skeleton of science. Manage Sci 2:197-208.

Durkin, J. (Ed.). (1981). Living Groups: Group Psychotherapy and General System Theory. New York: Bruner/Mazel.

Kielhofner, G. (1983). A paradigm for practice: The hierarchical organization of occupational therapy knowledge. In Health Through Occupation: Theory and Practice in Occupational Therapy. Philadelphia: F.A. Davis, pp.55-91.

Strauss, J., Loevsky, L., Glazer, W., Leaf, P. (1981). Organizing the complexities of schizophrenia. J Nerv Ment Dis 169(2):120-126.

von Bertalanffy, L. (1968). General System Theory: Foundations, Development, Applications. New York: George Braziller.

Theoretical Frameworks

Barris, R., Kielhofner, G., Watts, J. (1983). Psychosocial Occupational Therapy: Practice in a Pluralistic Arena. Laurel, MD: RAMSCO.

Bruce, M., Borg, B. (1987). Frames of Reference in Psychosocial Occupational Therapy. Thorofare, NJ: Charles B. Slack.

Cubie, S., Kaplan, K. (1982). A case analysis method for the model of human occupation. Am J Occup Ther 36(10):645-656.

Denton, P. (1986). Psychiatric Occupational Therapy: A Workbook of Practical Skills. Boston: Little, Brown & Co.

Mosey, A. (1970). Three Frames of Reference for Mental Health. Thorofare, NJ: Charles B. Slack.

CHAPTER 3

WHAT'S WRONG WITH THEM?

Identifying Patient Problems

The Five Languages

Now that we have covered the background of the Directive Group, the setting in which it was developed, and the predominate theoretical framework, we can look at practical ways to find patients who are appropriate for this type of treatment. Before addressing referral criteria, let's think about the different ways to identify patient problems. What you think is wrong with patients depends on your training, perspective, and what you are looking for. *Why* you think patients have the problems they do raises even more complex debates.

Outcomes of research findings provide multiple and often conflicting explanations of patient conditions. No matter what the reasons for mental illness, Directive Group patients still experience functional problems which greatly interfere with their competently engaging in daily routines. The Directive Group approach is congruent with patients' capacities, regardless of etiology. Group treatment does not ameliorate the underlying pathology; rather it offers patients an opportunity to derive satisfaction from and success in their immediate environment.

For the purposes of this book, I have focused primarily on the what and not the why questions. To identify patient problems I have organized sources of data into five categories and called them "languages," based on the special vocabulary common to each. These languages may help you plan a needs assessment by sorting information from different sources and by identifying tools for collecting such data.

Inner Experience

The first language is that of the Inner Experience. This is the patient's description of his or her thoughts, feelings, and perceptions. It is a subjective source in that only the patient can verify the experience based on introspection. Patient interviews are a common method of acquiring such information.

Behavioral Observation

To only use the patient's self-assessment would leave out a whole range of other available data. Another source of data is the patient's history. This is an example of Behavioral Observation. This assessment is based on what others, like family members, co-workers, or friends, have seen or heard the patient do or say. It is objective in that other people besides the patient can verify the information based on comparative observations. Observations made by staff on the unit or observations in a group by the co-leaders are a similar source of data in this category. These are actions which can be quantified and involve use of the senses to perceive them. A common assessment tool used in research and appropriate for Directive Group level patients is the Nurses Observation Scale for Inpatient Evaluation (NOSIE).[3]

Problem Oriented

A third type of language is based on the psychiatrist's training. This language is Problem Oriented and is based on an interpretation of the data from the first two languages. Psychiatrists are taught to assess mental functioning through an interview, with special questions designed to reveal impairments in a variety of areas, for example, the Mental Status Examination.[5] The results are reported through a list of symptoms and the degree of severity of the symptoms. A research instrument which tracks similar symptoms and could be used in a study of Directive Group is the Brief Psychiatric Rating Scale (BPRS).[4] A clinical source of data in this category is the master problem list. This list identifies the priority areas from the Mental Status Evaluation which form the basis for the treatment plan. These problems also help distinguish the areas dealt with in each of the specially designed treatment groups in a program.

Psychiatric Diagnosis

The fourth type of language is also based on the psychiatrist's training, the Psychiatric Diagnosis. This is the most refined classification of vocabulary published in the DSM III-R.[1] It is developed for clinicians and research investigators. The primary (axis I) psychiatric diagnosis is based on the assumption of the medical model approach to disease. However, there are four other axes which together give a multifaceted evaluation of the patient. The language which I am referring to is the axis I diagnosis, as it is the most frequently used diagnosis classification on medical records and is able to communicate in shorthand a composite picture of the patient's mental functioning. The criteria for each diagnosis is based on clusters of symptoms and behavioral observations. It represents a synthesis of the above three languages.

Theoretical Framework

The final type of language is based on the occupational therapist's training. This classification is usually determined by the therapist's theoretical framework. The profession also has a uniform terminology which may be used as well. The Theoretical Framework suggests categories for grouping observations in a similar way that the DSM III-R is categorized. However, our categories are not yet standardized in a manual as extensive or accepted as the DSM III-R. In addition, this language is based on information gathered from the patient and others which reveals the patient's occupational behavior — how the individual functions in everyday tasks and roles. Hypothetically, a person's adaptive functioning may not reveal a psychiatric disorder. Although in the hospital setting, almost every patient has both a psychiatric diagnosis and an occupational dysfunction. It should be noted, however, that although the psychiatric diagnosis will be identified, the occupational dysfunction often is not.

Identifying Patients for Directive Group

Use of Observation

The easiest way to identify patients for Directive Group is by the second language, by observing them on the unit — sitting in the lobby, staying in their rooms, eating meals. Many of the patients can't find their meal tray without assistance. They may need reminding to finish their food. They may not talk during the meals or participate in evening activities. They are inattentive to time, needing accompaniment to get to meetings. Some have trouble getting dressed independently. They tend to either sit alone and be passive or to be hyperactive and disturbing to others. They may provoke verbally aggressive encounters or interrupt conversations with their own unrelated thoughts. Sometimes they rush around in a flurry of seemingly unpurposeful activity, or they look agitated, shaking their leg continuously or grimacing.

By using your clinical judgment to list the behaviors most descriptive of these patients, you can establish referral criteria. Prioritize them by eliminating those problems not treatable in a short time frame. You can organize the list of behaviors by your theoretical framework and then write them so they are understandable by the staff on your unit. These behavioral observations serve as the screening tool for identifying the need for your services. The referral criteria will help determine as quickly as possible who could benefit from the Directive Group (Figure 3-1).

Just because you have referral criteria doesn't mean patients are automatically referred to the group. Entry to the group relies on interdisciplinary staff support. Usually the patient's primary nurse fills out the referral form based on his or her observations of the patient and his or her knowledge about this group. However, every staff member has multiple responsibilities, and ultimately group leaders are the most sensitive to patients who aren't in the group who need to be.

You need to be proactive in routinely reviewing the patients on the unit and asking the appropriate staff member to write a referral. This interaction

```
┌─────────────────────────────────────────────────────────────────────┐
│                      DIRECTIVE GROUP REFERRAL                         │
│          (Designed to Develop Adaptive Behavior and Basic Skills)     │
│                                                                       │
│   Recent History:  Work  _____                           │
│                                                                       │
│   Leisure _____                          │
│                                                                       │
│   Relationships _____        _____  │
│                                                     Addressograph     │
│                                                                       │
│                                                                       │
│   CIRCLE RELEVANT PROBLEM(S) FOR THIS PATIENT SPECIFIED ON MASTER     │
│   PROBLEM LIST                                                        │
│                                                                       │
│   #__  Disorientation, concrete thinking, decreased concentration    │
│   #__  Dependent on ADL, passive, helpless                           │
│   #__  Social withdrawal, negativistic, poor interactional skills    │
│   #__  Other _____ │
│                                                                       │
│                                                                       │
│   CHECK SPECIFIC AREAS OF DIFFICULTY FOR THIS PATIENT                 │
│                                                                       │
│   Inability to enact roles with others around a common task          │
│                                                                       │
│   __ rarely initiates verbal interactions with others                │
│   __ acts aggressively towards others with minimal provocation       │
│   __ infrequently or inappropriately responds to comments from others│
│   __ monopolizes interactions despite repeated feedback              │
│   __ passive, slowed involvement in activities with others           │
│   __ competitive, hyperactive involvement in activities with others  │
│                                                                       │
│   Inability to perform basic self maintenance habits                 │
│                                                                       │
│   __ consistently needs assistance to dress self appropriately in a.m.│
│   __ consistently needs assistance to follow daily time schedule     │
│                                                                       │
│   Inability to utilize basic cognitive and task skills               │
│                                                                       │
│   __ inability to focus on single task for more than 5 minutes       │
│   __ inability to plan and carry out a simple task without assistance │
│      (e.g., a familiar, 1-2 step process, e.g., finding meal tray)   │
│                                                                       │
│                                                                       │
│   Additional information about this patient relevant to participation Directive│
│   Group: _____ │
│                                                                       │
│   _____ │
│                                                                       │
│   Goals of referral: _____ │
│                                                                       │
│   _____ │
│                                                                       │
│                                                                       │
│   Staff Signature _____        Date _____   │
└─────────────────────────────────────────────────────────────────────┘
```

Figure 3-1. Directive Group Referral Form.
From The George Washington University Medical Center Inpatient Unit, 1983.

is a place for informal inservice education, since you may be explaining your thinking about the patient and the group therapy program to someone unfamiliar with this system. To the extent you handle these negotiations with diplomacy, the patients receive treatment faster and more effectively. The staff members generally give the patient the first introduction to what the group is about and why they were referred. You get a chance to reinforce and expand on this message once the patient comes to group.

Typical Patients Referred to Directive Group

Patients referred to Directive Group can be described in many ways. The patients may report unusual sensations, feelings, or thoughts or have difficulty explaining much of their inner experience. Their history generally reveals a recent change in behavior with a profound inability to function. The Mental Status Examination (Problem-Oriented language) will frequently list severe symptoms, such as hallucinations, hyperactivity or psychomotor retardation, concrete thinking, loose associations, tangentiality, extreme mood disturbance, apathy, dependence, memory deficits, indecisiveness, and impaired insight and judgment.

Patients referred to Directive Group often have a psychiatric diagnosis of a schizophrenic disorder (catatonic or paranoid type or schizophreniform), organic brain syndrome (or toxic psychosis), major depressive disorder, or bipolar disorder (manic, depressed, or mixed). These may be acute episodes or recurrent.

On the unit, based on behavioral observation, these patients ranging in age from adolescent to elderly show marked difficulty attending to simple tasks, following a schedule or self-care routine, and engaging in conversations. They show extreme behavior — either passive or hyperactive, withdrawn or monopolizing, helpless or aggressive, confused or resistant.

In the language of the model of human occupation (Theoretical Framework), these patients feel out of control, expect failure, avoid mastery experiences, and fear exploring their environment. Volitionally, they have difficulty identifying interests and goals and show little pleasure in activities. As characterized by their habituation subsystem, they have no primary role to organize their day. Their current habits of self-care and time management are markedly disrupted. According to the performance subsystem, they have extremely limited interpersonal (communication/interaction) skills and task-oriented skills (both process and motor).

It doesn't matter exactly how you describe these patients. What matters is that you know them when you see them and you know how to describe them to the staff with whom you work. Then you will also be clear on who doesn't need the group. One shorthand and new way to identify these patients is to use the Global Assessment Functioning Scale, axis V of the DSM III-R (Table 3-1).[2] Patients with a global assessment of 11 to 20 and 21 to 30 points would qualify for referral. Patients scoring 1 to 10 would be excluded as they would probably be in a quiet room or require one-on-one supervision and find the group setting over stimulating. Similarly, patients with 31 to 40 points would probably not be referred to the group because they could be evaluated by a greater range of occupational therapy tools than behavioral observation and could begin to collaborate in the treatment process through groups organized at the competence level.

Case Example — Fred

Directive Group is one part of the inpatient service delivery of care. The occupational therapy process is similar to the treatment process of most professions and is coordinated with the overall goals of inpatient hospitaliza-

---

Global Assessment of Functioning Scale (GAF Scale)

Consider psychological, social, and occupational functioning on a hypothetical continuum of mental health-illness. Do not include impairment in functioning due to physical (or environmental) limitations. See p. 20 for instructions on how to use this scale.

Note: Use intermediate codes when appropriate, e.g., 45, 68, 72.

Code

Code	
90 | 81	**Absent or minimal symptoms** (e.g., mild anxiety before an exam), **good functioning in all areas, interested and involved in a wide range of activities, socially effective, generally satisfied with life, no more than everyday problems or concerns** (e.g., an occasional argument with family members).
80 | 71	**If symptoms are present, they are transient and expectable reactions to psychosocial stressors** (e.g., difficulty concentrating after family argument); **no more than slight impairment in social, occupational, or school functioning** (e.g., temporarily falling behind in school work).
70 | 61	**Some mild symptoms** (e.g., depressed mood and mild insomnia) **OR some difficulty in social, occupational, or school functioning** (e.g., occasional truancy, or theft within the household), **but generally functioning pretty well, has some meaningful interpersonal relationships.**
60 | 51	**Moderate symptoms** (e.g., flat affect and circumstantial speech, occasional panic attacks) **OR moderate difficulty in social, occupational, or school functioning** (e.g., few friends, conflicts with co-workers).
50 | 41	**Serious symptoms** (e.g., suicidal ideation, severe obsessional rituals, frequent shoplifting) **OR any serious impairment in social, occupational, or school functioning** (e.g., no friends, unable to keep a job).
40 | 31	**Some impairment in reality testing or communication** (e.g., speech is at times illogical, obscure, or irrelevant) **OR major impairment in several areas, such as work or school, family relations, judgment, thinking, or mood** (e.g., depressed man avoids friends, neglects family, and is unable to work; child frequently beats up younger children, is defiant at home, and is failing at school).
30 | 21	**Behavior is considerably influenced by delusions or hallucinations OR serious impairment in communication or judgment** (e.g., sometimes incoherent, acts grossly inappropriately, suicidal preoccupation) **OR inability to function in almost all areas** (e.g., stays in bed all day; no job, home, or friends).
20 | 11	**Some danger of hurting self or others** (e.g., suicide attempts without clear expectation of death, frequently violent, manic excitement) **OR occasionally fails to maintain minimal personal hygiene** (e.g., smears feces) **OR gross impairment in communication** (e.g., largely incoherent or mute).
10 | 1	**Persistent danger of severely hurting self or others** (e.g., recurrent violence) **OR persistent inability to maintain minimal personal hygiene OR serious suicidal act with clear expectation of death.**

Table 3-1. DSM-III Axis V Diagnosis
From Endicott, J., Spitzer, R., Fleiss, J. (1987). Global assessment of functioning scale. In: DSM-IIIR: Diagnostic and Statistical Manual of Mental Disorders, 3rd ed. revised. Washington, D.C.: American Psychiatric Association.

tion. The process includes: screening, evaluation, treatment planning, treatment implementation, monitoring progress, and termination. To illustrate how the group is integrated into the comprehensive treatment program, let's follow a patient from admission to discharge. The focus is on the different ways of gathering data (screening) which leads to a referral to the group. This case example also provides a flavor of the group (treatment planning and implementation) from an individual patient perspective. The next chapter looks at the group from the perspective of the group as a whole.

Fred came into the emergency room Sunday night escorted by his wife.

Patient Assessment

Subjective Data (Inner Experience) Fred told the physician he felt that he was being attacked by insects, that bugs were sucking on his brain. For the past two to three weeks he noted less self-confidence and energy. He said he was afraid to take his hypertensive medication because he thought they might be poisoning him. He described less will to live.

Objective Data (Behavioral Observation). His wife of 47 years said that over the past few weeks he had difficulty falling asleep and awoke early. He recently lost 20 pounds and quit his job as a security guard. He is 71 and had no previous psychiatric history.

Mental Status Evaluation (Problem Oriented). The admitting psychiatrist reported that the patient appeared sad and worried, and his affect was depressed and anxious. His behavior revealed withdrawal, passivity, and dependency. His motor activity was decreased. His speech was reduced and slowed. He had difficulty with concentration and had memory deficits.

Observations on the Unit (Behavioral Observation). Fred's primary nurse observed him on the unit in the evening and the next morning. She noted he was unable to find his meal tray without assistance and needed reminding to continue eating after every few minutes. He hardly responded to attempts to include him in conversation. He was slow and passive when walking down the hall or sitting in the lobby.

Axis I Diagnosis (Psychiatric Diagnosis). His team psychiatrist gave him the DSM III diagnosis of major depressive disorder. This was based on his prominent and persistent dysphoric mood (i.e., depressed, sad, hopeless). In addition, he met the criteria for having at least four of the seven symptoms listed for at least two weeks (significant weight loss, insomnia, psychomotor retardation, loss of interest in usual activities, fatigue, feelings of worthlessness, diminished ability to concentrate, and suicidal ideation).

Master Problem List (Problem Oriented). By the time the afternoon staff team met, there was sufficient information about Fred to begin his treatment plan and enter it in his chart, the permanent medical record. The 6 North unit uses the problem-oriented recordkeeping method developed by Weed.[6] After the psychiatrist reviewed the patient's history, Mental Status Examination results, and physical examination, the nursing staff gave their observations. Other staff on the team asked questions for clarification and then came up with an initial master problem list:
1. Depressed mood
2. Delusional thinking
3. Passivity.

Treatment Plan

With the major problems listed, the next step was to identify the therapeutic activities which would address these problems and help the patient improve. For depressed mood, Fred would be seen individually by his psychiatrist for short daily sessions. The patient would meet with his primary nurse or the nurse covering for her for 15-minute checks throughout the day. He was scheduled for a family therapy meeting later in the week with the social worker to gather further information and offer support. As soon as his lab work and other evaluations were complete, he would be started on a trial of antidepressant medication (Nortriptyline, 25 mg). Because of his delusional thinking and other cognitive impairments noted on the Mental Status Examination, he was given a work-up for dementia. A diagnosis of organic brain syndrome was eventually ruled out based on a normal neurologic exam, favorable response to antidepressant medication, and absence of a specific organic etiologic factor. His cognitive impairments resolved as his mood improved.

Referral to Directive Group

Fred was given a structured schedule to follow and referred to Directive Group (Figure 3-2). The relevant problem from the master problem list was passivity. The behaviors which indicated this problem were that he rarely initiated verbal interactions with others, and he had passive, slowed involvement in activities with others. He also had an inability to focus on a single task for more than five minutes and an inability to plan and carry out a simple task without assistance. These were behaviors, which if monitored over time, could contribute to making a differential diagnosis between dementia and depression.

Participation in Directive Group

When Fred first came to Directive Group, he was in pajamas and complained he couldn't do anything. He was given the goal of getting dressed before group, which the nursing staff helped him do. Within the group he could imitate movements and all of his attempts to participate were supported. He was also given the task of changing the arrow on the large calendar to the correct date each day. This gave him a specific role which helped him stay oriented to time and to get positive feedback for completing his task.

As previously discussed, he initially looked like someone who might have organicity because of his passivity, confusion, and helplessness. Part of the goal of referral to Directive Group was to help differentiate his possible psychiatric diagnosis of major depressive disorder v. organic brain syndrome. We reported on his responsiveness to small goals and support, and the absence of indicators of perceptual dysfunction on tasks such as drawing a large self-portrait or copying a design for a tile tray. This information, coupled with feedback from other staff members and the results of neurological testing, which recommended a full treatment for depression before reevaluating dementia, helped the psychiatrist to decide to prescribe antidepressant medication.

```
                    DIRECTIVE GROUP REFERRAL
        (Designed to Develop Adaptive Behavior and Basic Skills)


Recent History:  Work  quit- security guard

Leisure  _____        Fred

Relationships  married  47 yrs  _____
                                          Addressograph


CIRCLE RELEVANT PROBLEM(S) FOR THIS PATIENT SPECIFIED ON MASTER
PROBLEM LIST

#__  Disorientation, concrete thinking, decreased concentration
#✓  Dependent on ADL, (passive) helpless
#__  Social withdrawal, negativistic, poor interactional skills
#__  Other  _____


CHECK SPECIFIC AREAS OF DIFFICULTY FOR THIS PATIENT

Inability to enact roles with others around a common task

✓ rarely initiates verbal interactions with others
__ acts aggressively towards others with minimal provocation
__ infrequently or inappropriately responds to comments from others
__ monopolizes interactions despite repeated feedback
✓ passive, slowed involvement in activities with others
__ competitive, hyperactive involvement in activities with others

Inability to perform basic self maintenance habits

__ consistently needs assistance to dress self appropriately in a.m.
__ consistently needs assistance to follow daily time schedule

Inability to utilize basic cognitive and task skills

✓ inability to focus on single task for more than 5 minutes
✓ inability to plan and carry out a simple task without assistance
   (e.g., a familiar, 1-2 step process, e.g., finding meal tray)


Additional information about this patient relevant to participation Directive

Group:  Pt. has exhibited delusional thinking,
        some incontinence.

Goals of referral:  ↑ social interaction + independence.
        Help evaluate cognitive impairments.



Staff Signature  _____    Date  _____
```

Figure 3-2. Directive Group Referral Form — Fred.

By the end of the second week, Fred was discharged from Directive Group, after having attended nine sessions, and referred to Task Group, Exercise Group, and Activity Planning for Evening Activities. During the last few sessions he had been able to attend to Directive Group for the full 45 minutes and cooperate on the activities without assistance. In his soft-spoken manner he spontaneously made jokes about the activities and gave the instructions for playing a word game. He fully engaged the attention of the group when doing a modified charade portraying an airplane. He was back to being well groomed, social, and interested in living.

Fred was discharged from the hospital, continuing his medications, to his home with his wife a week later. He came back to visit the unit after a month wearing his security guard uniform, having gotten back his previous job. Seeing his progress provided the staff with a "return on their investment" that we don't often get because of not having a built-in system of follow-up. He also provided an example to counteract the myths many people, even students and new therapists, find themselves believing about aging. Not all elderly patients are organic, destined to be discharged to a nursing home and not able to work or give pleasure to others.

References

1. DSM-IIIR: Diagnostic and Statisitical Manual of Mental Disorders, 3rd ed. revised. (1987). Washington, DC: American Psychiatric Association.
2. Endicott, J., Spitzer, R., Fleiss, J. (1987). Global assessment of functioning scale. In DSM-IIIR: Diagnostic and Statistical Manual of Mental Disorders, 3rd ed. revised. Washington, DC: American Psychiatric Association.
3. Honigfeld, G., Klett, C. (1965). The Nurses Observation Scale for Inpatient Evaluation. J Clin Psychol 21:65-71.
4. Overall, J., Gorham, D. (1962). The Brief Psychiatric Rating Scale. Psychol Reports 10:799-812).
5. Psychiatric History and Mental Status Examination. (1981). In Kaplan H., Sadock, B.: Modern Synopsis of Comprehensive Textbook of Psychiatry III. Baltimore: Williams & Wilkins, pp. 185-205.
6. Weed, L. (1971). Medical Records, Medical Evaluation, and Patient Care. Chicago: Year Book Medical Publishers.

Suggested Reading

Hertzman, M. (1984). Inpatient Psychiatry: Toward Rapid Restoration of Function. New York: Human Services Press.

Hopkins, H. & Tiffany, E. (1983). Occupational Therapy — A problem-solving process. In H. Hopkins & H. Smith (Eds.) Williard & Spackman's Occupational Therapy (6th ed). (pp. 89-99) Philadelphia: Lippincott.

Rogers, J. (1982). Order and disorder in medicine and occupational therapy. Am J Occup Ther 36(1):29-35.

CHAPTER 4

WHAT'S THERE TO DO?
Planning Group Activities

Rationale for Planning

Every group takes planning. Even if you change your plan halfway through the group or disband it altogether, you need a plan first to help guide your actions. When new to a situation, group leaders handle their nervousness in different ways. Some want to just see how it goes, using the "fly by the seat of the pants" method. Others react by trying to control things and predict what might occur. This second group of people will be relieved by having a plan. The first group will need to try both approaches, with and without planning, to see why plans are important.

In general, winging it only makes sense for a very experienced clinician who has integrated the principles we are about to describe. Once you have a history of being thoroughly prepared to do a wide range of interventions, you can be spontaneous. Then, when you feel as if you are making it up as you go along, you realize you are finally demonstrating the artistry which results from lots of hard work, preparation and planning, and learning from mistakes.

Leading a group from a position of strength requires knowledge. As we discussed in Chapter 1, on a general level you need to know group dynamics, be self-aware, and understand behavior patterns. But on a specific treatment level, you need to know who the patients are, what the goals for them include, and the overall purpose of the group. Within this context you plan the day's activities.

Just as in research you have a hypothesis that you test out through an experiment and then conclude whether your original ideas were rejected or supported by the results, so too in leading a group you test your ideas against your observations.

Rationale for the Sequence of Events

All types of therapy groups, including higher level, functionally oriented activity groups and verbal group psychotherapy, have a sequence of events or go through stages of development within a session. There is always some time spent getting the group oriented to the purpose of the group and getting ready to work together. Some groups use warm-up activities, such as nonverbal exercises, to get the group going. Others warm up in an evolving, unplanned way, through the flow of discussion. There is always a middle section focusing on the topic, task, or process of the session. This leads to the ending of the session when a sense of closure is drawn. Sometimes the group reviews what it did and tries to understand their dynamics. Other times the group plans what it will focus on next time it meets.

In Directive Group, because of the short attention spans and memory impairments of many of the members, each session is complete within itself. Even though the leaders may be thinking about the next session and see some continuity for planning, this is not shared with the patients in the wrap-up.

In higher level groups patients can focus on one activity or concentrate on a conversation among the members for an hour. In Directive Group, since this is not the case, the activities need to be short and continuously changing. They need not all relate to a single theme. The structure of the group provides the continuity and coherence. Planning the activities like this is more of a challenge for the leaders initially than the patients. It will probably feel as though you are pulling from all the groups you used to run separately and putting them all in one session which, in a sense, you are. The guideline to move from movement to objects to people is based on developmental principles of how children learn through play.[1] Because Directive Group patients are temporarily functioning at minimal levels, this sequence helps support the relearning of basic skills, starting with the most familiar and simple and increasing involvement through the more challenging and complex.

Where Do You Start?

You start with the most recent information. If it is your first group ever, or if you have mostly new patients starting the group, you base your plans on observations of patients on the ward, in other groups or informal settings. Most likely, you are leading an ongoing group, in which case you base your plans on the group experience of the previous day. If during yesterday's group there was a fairly active energy level, evidence of concentrating on a series of short activities, and continuity of group membership, then you would build from there. You would expect the group to respond to the same types and amounts of activities. You would alter the content slightly to provide variation, but keep the components similar to provide familiarity.

Structuring the Session and Sample Activities

All groups have a content and structure. The content of Directive Group defies easy categorization because it includes a wide range of activities (occupations) appropriate for the development of basic skills. The group is structured around a sequence of events. When planning, first think through each segment and analyze the activities for each part individually. Then, before plunging ahead, review the sequence as a cohesive whole.

All groups also have a place to meet. Directive Group should have a consistent location, large enough for tables and chairs, and with a door to provide privacy and security. If you don't have such a room, find other ways to establish boundaries for the group. With patients who are easily distracted and fearful, it is very important to help them focus and feel safe. Using concrete objects and performing activities assist in this regard. We rely heavily on the blackboard, posters of individual goals, the clock, and a large balloon. (Organizing space is addressed in Chapter 6, and the environment is discussed in Chapter 9.)

Orientation

The first part is always the orientation to the group. Usually it is helpful to engage one of the first people who enter the group at the blackboard. Choose someone who has been in the group before and can be somewhat organized when given individual cues. Decide what you are going to write on the board and what blanks you want the patient to fill in. For example, the following format might be used:

This is _____ Group. Today is _____. The month and year are _____. The purpose of the group is _____

_____.

One possible purpose statement is "to help you learn to take care of yourself as much as possible." Another is "to learn to be more self-directed."

You might review the four overall goals of the group (discussed in Chapter 5) at this point, or keep them in mind and refer to them later. A large poster of ten individual goals (described in Chapter 6) is used to give examples to the patients. Even though logically goal-setting would seem to come during the orientation to the group, the attention span of most of the members of this group is such that they will not easily take in verbal activity. If they do attend to conversation, it is usually based on here and now concrete experience that is short in length and interactively based. Therefore, the beginning of the group usually changes rather quickly (5 minutes or less) into the most basic and familiar type of activity, simple movement chosen to stimulate at least a reflexive response.

Introduction

The next part of the group involves the introduction of new members and a review of everyone's name. This is easily accomplished through throwing a large red balloon and saying the name of the person to whom you are throwing the balloon each time. You can alter this by increasing the speed, passing the balloon in a circle in order, or having people state their own names first as they pass the balloon.

The leader's job is to carefully monitor the patients' responses and alter the activity as needed. In the above example, if everyone seems to catch on to each other's name fairly quickly and also to like the balloon, then add categories when you throw the balloon. For instance, ask everyone to say the name of a car when they get the balloon. When that wears out, try flowers or fruits.

If the patients seem overly taxed by the cognitive demands of categories, but responsive to the movement part of the game, then just have them try to keep the balloon in the air as long as possible. You might start counting each time someone hits it, starting over when it hits the ground. It is important to make the game fun and not evoke a sense that they could fail, for example, by not hitting it enough times. Getting to ten may be high enough.

The Introduction takes about 5 to 10 minutes.

Warm-up Activities

The next part is warm-up activities. These lead naturally from the balloon game. Depending on how much time is devoted to the balloon, these can be curtailed or elaborated, from 5 to 10 minutes. Often simple physical exercises are useful in continuing to engage the members' attention and interest. If the group was energized from the balloon, then maybe they would all stand in a circle and one by one lead an exercise. Usually the leader starts as a way to set the tone and show exactly what is intended. The leader may say, for example, "Let's first raise our arms in the air and then lower them to our sides. Let's do it three more times. One, two, three. Good. Robert, your turn. Do you want to do something with your hands or your head?"

By giving structured choices, the patients are cued to follow the instructions and at the same time show some initiative. You always want to make the patients feel safe to get involved. You vary the structure depending on each individual's capacity. Someone who is obviously tuned into the activity could be given an open choice, such as "What type of exercise do you want to lead?" If, after a few turns, patients have caught on, they do not need cueing except if they do not realize it is their turn. If only one person is very confused, then give that person more assistance, but in a kind supportive way so the other patients do not feel impatient or ashamed for that individual. If one patient is nonverbal and doesn't seem able to pay attention to the activity, then look for a chance movement and use it as the exercise, for instance, a yawn, a scratch, or even a blink. "Rose, I saw you blink. We haven't done that one today. Let's everyone blink real hard. Open, close, now open your eyes." Sometimes that gets the nonverbal patient to laugh or at least give you eye contact and indicate some connection. In any case, it keeps everyone involved and prevents the activity from getting bogged down. If others start to lose interest or appear distracted, you know you better move on to a new activity altogether.

Selected Activities

The selected activity or activities for the day are next. You may need a series of short ones or one long one. This could take from 10 to 20 minutes. Consider the motor, cognitive, and interaction needs you are aiming to match and develop. Usually the group moves to a game at this point which incorporates simple rules and movement with an object, because games build on the movement aspects previously accomplished and add a cognitive and interactive component.

A wide range of games with a ball can be used here. If the previous day you played modified basketball (throwing the Nerf ball into a basket in the center of the circle), maybe today you want to try sit-down soccer (kicking the Nerf ball between the chairs in a circle.) If the game gets an active response, which it usually does, then you may want to have people stand up and play bean bag toss.

If the attention span seems to be building, you may use this observation as a clue for planning the following day's activity, for instance, a longer activity of modified bowling (using large plastic soda bottles decorated as pins, which could be made by patients in a higher level group.) This game can use the skills of a patient who is attuned to rules and numbers to keep score, such as an adolescent who is showing negativity, a paranoid patient who wants to keep some distance, or a patient who is slightly bored because he or she is ready to leave the group and needs more challenge.

Wrap-up

When about ten minutes remain to the group, you begin the wrap-up activities. This phase provides meaning to the activities and a sense of closure for the session. Patients gather their chairs together, facing the blackboard. To make the transition to this quieter part of the group, you first may do a word game, such as guessing the word for which you have placed the appropriate amount of letters. Tell the group what category it is in; it may be a patient's name in the group, an activity the group played today, or something you saw some people do during the session.

For example, L A U G H

Then you might ask the patients to name in order all the activities you did during the session while you write them down. Then you could have them vote on which one they liked the best, which one they would like to do again, or which one they thought was the hardest.

It is important to pay attention to which members are leaving the group. Patients frequently come and go, and each patient's contribution needs to be acknowledged as a way to make people feel valued. You also strive to provide continuity with the remaining core of the group who may otherwise feel unduly disrupted by the changing membership. Sometimes patients are given a certificate of participation or a graduation award. Other times they review the goals they were working on and met, which are posted on a bulletin board or written on a card. As with every other part of the group, this activity is analyzed by the leader to match the needs and capacities of the individual member.

Post-Group Session

After the group there is a 15-minute post-group session for the co-leaders, which is held in the same room as the group. This should be scheduled as a regularly occurring part of the group. Any additional staff and students who were in the group for the day should be included in the discussion. The co-leaders use this time for several functions:

-To discuss the group as a whole — for instance, how well the plan went, the adaptations which were made, the mood of the group and possible reasons for it, and how the group changed from beginning to end

-To discuss the roles the co-leaders took and any problems in communication that need to be addressed

-To plan what to do in the group the next day and assign responsibility for preparations

-To assess individual patient behavior by filling out the rating scale which is posted in the nurses station (discussed more in Chapter 5)

-To decide any additional information that needs to be communicated to other staff, either during the next team meeting or to the nursing staff immediately after the post-group session.

References

1. Robinson, A. (1971). Play: The arena for acquisition of rules for competent behavior. Am J Occup Ther 31(4):248-253.

Suggested Reading and Resources

Boyd, N. (1975). Handbook of Recreational Games: How to Play More Than 300 Children's Games. New York: Dover.

Capon, J. (1975). Perceptual Motor Development: Tire, Parachute Activities. Belmont, CA: Fearon.

Fluegelman, A. (1976). The New Games Book. San Francisco: The Headlands Press.

Remocker, A., Storch E. (1983). Action Speaks Louder: A Handbook for Nonverbal Group Techniques, 3rd ed. New York: Churchill Livingstone.

S&S Arts and Crafts Catalog. (1987). Colchester, CT 06145. (203) 537-3451.

CHAPTER 5

WHY ARE WE DOING THIS?
Establishing Group Goals

This chapter begins with why group goals are necessary. Goals are viewed from the larger context of the health care system to the goals of hospitalization and of specific groups within the program. For example, the goals of verbal group therapy are contrasted with the goals of Directive Group. Then the four group goals of Directive Group are elaborated in terms of how they are expressed through the behavior of the group members and how the goals relate to the theoretical framework. The chapter goes on to describe how the goals are operationalized for assessing individual behavior, monitoring patient progress, and documenting the achievement of group goals. A case example demonstrates the use of these procedures.

Why Have Group Goals?

All treatment groups have goals. Most group therapy goals encompass the learnings to be engaged in by all of the members. For instance, the goal might be to develop authentic communication or to help each other abstain from self-destructive behavior. While an individual may have several motives for joining a group, he or she usually understands that the common denominator is addressing each other's emotional needs.

Directive Group patients, on the other hand, initially don't have the capacity to identify with such group goals or needs. Therefore, the group goals are adapted to enable the patients to develop basic skills required to begin to interact with each other in the same room.

Goals are important for the following reasons:

-To be clear about how to lead the group to meet the goals.

-To help patients understand why they are in the group and what to focus on.

-To communicate to other staff why you have the group, so you can get appropriate referrals and interdisciplinary support. Communication occurs informally, in team meetings, and formally, during inservice presentations.

-To be able to have the group purpose understood by supervisors, hospital administrators, or anyone else involved with evaluating the value of your program.

-To measure outcome and document accountability for results.

-To disseminate information to other potential leaders of the group, within and without your facility, serving a training and educational function.

The Big Picture

Patients who are admitted to an inpatient unit have selected one of the resources available for mental health care in their community. Ideally, there should be a range of facilities which offer services for people with mental disorders, both acute and chronic, of all ages and abilities to pay. This service delivery system should be coordinated to make possible continuity of care for patients with psychiatric problems. Unfortunately, this is not always the case. For instance, although there are many general hospitals with acute psychiatric units, and some day-treatment and outpatient programs, there are too few community programs which allow for extended follow-up.

There are many people in their community who don't have emotional problems requiring psychiatric services. The continuum stretches from the type of behavior that gets someone admitted to an acute psychiatric inpatient unit — such as a suicide attempt, inability to function due to depression or drug abuse, or not being able to take care of oneself due to organic brain syndrome or psychosis — to the type of behavior that keeps people out of the system, such as the ability to function adaptively in one's home, work, and community environment (Table 5-1).

The net result of this range of problems is that the acute care unit admits patients with varying functional needs, backgrounds, diagnoses, and ages. Because of the complex nature of psychosocial dysfunction, many different types of services are offered, from pharmacology to psychotherapy. The key ingredient is an individualized approach to patient care. This may be pro-

Type of Service	Inpatient Hospitalization				Day Treatment and Community	Out-Patient	No Need for M.H. Services
Example of Treatment	Quiet Room	Directive Group	Task Group	Discharge Planning Group	Transitional Employment	Stress Management	Self-Analysis
Focus of Treatment	Survival	Skills	Habits	Roles	Community Adjustment	Enhancing Meaning	Self-Discovery

Table 5-1. Continuum of Mental Health Services.

vided through individual therapy or group therapy. In a group program each group provides graded opportunities for patients to develop the skills, habits, and roles necessary for productive living in their expected environments. Each group requires realistic and explicit goals.

For instance, the goals of inpatient verbal group therapy might encourage patients to:
-Identify their own issues to address in the group.
-Respond to others with empathy and honesty.
-Work on making personal changes within the group.
-Take risks to reveal feelings and fears as they come up.

Clearly these goals require an individual to have more psychological integration, less overwhelming anxiety, and better adaptive functioning than patients in Directive Group. That doesn't mean that these higher level group therapy patients don't have their own immense needs. They may have problems with substance abuse, be unable to keep a job, or have extreme marital difficulties. Nevertheless, they are able to talk about these problems and benefit from thinking through coping strategies.

Usually, after participating in Directive Group, patients recompensate from the acute phase of their illness. Then, they too can begin this work. However, our experience and current research has shown more and more Directive Group patients are chronically disabled. This means that their illness presents with multiple acute exacerbations and that their functioning does not approach the degree of health needed to participate in insight oriented therapy. Rather, these patients benefit from structured group approaches which develop needed skills, such as social skill training, leisure education, and vocational readiness. Some of the more functional patients may focus on assertiveness training, changing their leisure lifestyles, and developing their work role. Although each of these groups would have a different emphasis for goals, they assume a similar level of functioning.

Group Goals for Minimally Functioning Individuals

Now let us return to the types of goals that elicit more adpative behavior from minimally functioning adults. The Directive Group goals are established to articulate this desired state of patient interactions within the group. The goals identify the type of behavior the treatment approach is attempting to augment or diminish. As outcome goals, they indicate the criteria for successful achievement within the group session. As process goals, they indicate the functions provided by the group leaders to elicit the expected outcomes. (The roles of the co-leaders will be further discussed in chapter 7.) If you are focusing on the group goals, then you will provide activities in which the patients can participate. You will encourage task-oriented verbal interaction. You will be sure to keep the established time boundaries, and you will make room during the flow of the group for patients to initiate activity ideas.

Then, after the group, you and the co-leaders can assess whether the activities and interactions actually supported the group goals. Was there time for each activity? Were the chosen activities harmonious with each other? Did they involve the patients optimally? What would you do differently if you had the chance to redo the group session, knowing what you know now? Which activities would you repeat in the future? Did the activities stimulate ideas for further adaptations or new activities all together?

A patient is ready to be discharged from Directive Group when he or she is able to:

-Participate in the activities of each session.
-Interact verbally with others around the common tasks.
-Attend the group consistently.
-Initiate activities within the group.

Participation

Participate in the activities of each session refers to the nonverbal ways patients can be involved in the group, essentially through thinking and doing. Patients may not respond to conversation but still do the warm-up exercises. Initially they may be slow and passive, but eventually show active involvement. Or the patients may be able to imitate movements but not follow instructions for a simple two step craft.

This goal relates to the performance subsystem of the model of human occupation. Specifically it focuses on process (cognitive) skills and motor skills (perceptual motor, gross and fine motor). The cognitive skills are very basic. These patients are not expected to do abstract problem solving. Usually the tasks are familiar and have one to two steps or the steps are presented one at a time until each one is accomplished. There is room for a patient who is more organized cognitively to do more complex thinking within an activity (for instance, a patient who is familiar with a card game and can explain it, or suggest a way to plan a relay and organize the group into teams).

Likewise, the motor skills are basic. The gross motor skills require minimal endurance, strength, flexibility, and coordination. Fine motor skills are also kept to a minimum. Writing and cutting are used on craft tasks infrequently, and pinch and grasp used during games do not require great precision. Perceptual motor skills are prerequisite to and incorporated in gross and fine movements. When indications of problems occur, such as with reversals, rotations, or spatial relations, patients are referred for formal testing.

Interaction

Interact verbally with others around a common task refers to ways patients communicate with each other during the activities of the session. The emphasis is on talking. Since the primary medium for eliciting organized behavior is action, the verbal interaction is in conjunction with the activities patients do in the group. Patients may give a leader eye contact when he or she is explaining the activity, but not respond with words to a direct question. Sometimes patients do respond, but in a manner that is tangential, idiosyncratic, or incoherent. Other patients try to monopolize.

Verbal interaction relates to the communication/interaction skills of the performance subsystem. The level of communication expected in the group is basic. Patients can be expected to say their names during the introductory phase, to give appropriate responses during games requiring speaking, and answer questions during the wrap-up. Hopefully, patients get to the point where they can spontaneously ask questions and respond to comments. Patients are not expected to self-disclose feelings, give each other feedback, or role play social skills as these skills would be developed in higher level groups.

Attention

Attend the group consistently refers to the expectation that patients come to group on time and dressed. Initially, most of them aren't able to do this without assistance from staff. Usually a patient's primary nurse or nurse assigned for the shift will remind the patient about group or help him or her get dressed, unless the patient is restricted to hospital pajamas.

Attention to time is part of the habituation subsystem. Adaptive functioning in daily life roles requires that individuals can use their time effectively, appropriately, and with flexibility. But patients in Directive Group may be so distractable, confused, or disoriented that they may not even know the day of the week. That is why each group starts with orienting information. The group structure supports the patients in learning habits of punctuality and consistent attendance by meeting at a routine time and place. Attention to time is also emphasized throughout the group by encouraging patients to focus their attention for increasing increments of time.

Initiation

Initiate activities within the group refers to opportunities, provided by the leaders, for spontaneous, self-directed involvement from patients during a session. Again, this is at a most basic level. One way a patient can take initiative is to indicate his or her preference when offered a choice between two alternatives, such as doing exercises sitting or standing. Another way is to help explain the directions for an activity. The most initiative usually seen is making a suggestion for a game to play.

Initiation relates to the volitional subsystem. According to the model, this is conceptualized as the components which determine choices for occupational behavior. Humans are thought to be energized by an urge to master and explore the world. However, this is precisely what patients in Directive Group seem to have lost; they seem unmotivated, resistant, and fearful.

The Directive Group tries to elicit this urge through the stimulating, supportive, safe environment that is created. Specifically, patients are helped to realize the effects of their actions and the belief in their skills (personal causation) through feedback. Interests are solicited through the activities, choices, and wrap-up. By beginning to re-experience pleasure in activities, patients are more open to finding some meaning in their lives, if only fleeting. They are helped to identify what they value, by being treated with value and respect. Through focusing on individualized goals, they start to have a future perspective and take small steps towards competence. Through engaging the volitional subsystem, patients can initiate a basic role in the group. (How goals are individualized will be addressed in the next chapter.)

Operationalizing Goals

The leaders use the four goals of Directive Group to focus their observations during the session, to monitor patient progress after each session, and to evaluate when someone is ready to leave the group.

Evaluation

Discharge planning starts on admission in the short-term setting. For patients who have basic skills and are identified as needing in-depth evalua-

```
                          DIRECTIVE GROUP
                       Baseline Assessment Form
Referral problem(s):  #
S- (What patient said, characteristic statement)

O- PLEASE INDICATE APPROPRIATE RATINGS AND DESCRIPTIONS OF PATIENT'S BEHAVIOR:

                                                                          Not
                                              No    Partially   Yes    Observed
Basic Components of Volitional Subsystem
o  Patient identifies personal interests       1        2        3         X
o  Patient demonstrates goal-directed
   behavior                                    1        2        3         X
o  Patient demonstrates evidence of
   pleasure in activities, spontaneity,
   and anticipation of success.                1        2        3         X
Comments: (e.g. interests, goals, and motivation)

Basic Role Behaviors
o  Patient participates actively in each       1        2        3         X
   activity
o  Patient initiates one task related          1        2        3         X
   comment/or makes one comment at a time
o  Patient helps lead an activity              1        2        3         X
Comments: (e.g. manner/content of interaction, affect and coping skills)

Basic Self-Maintenance Habits
o  Patient is dressed in street clothes        1        2        3         X
   prior to beginning of session
o  Patient attends group on time               1        2        3         X
Comments: (e.g. appearance, response to time expectations)

Basic Cognitive Skills
o  Patient is able to stay in session          1        2        3         X
   for duration of group
o  Patient is able to focus attention          1        2        3         X
   for at least 25 minutes
o  Patient is able to follow instructions      1        2        3         X
   on simple tasks
o  Patient is able to explain directions       1        2        3         X
Comments: (e.g. fine, gross, and perceptual motor skills, elaborate on cognitive skills)

A- Assess patient's adaptive and maladaptive responses, areas of basic competence,
   comparison of current performance with past history, environmental requirements
   necessary to elicit adequate occupational behavior at this level.



P- Participate in the activities and relationships of Directive group for at least
   one week to work on the following short-term goal(s):




                                        _____
                                        Signature and Discipline's Initials
```

Figure 5-1. Directive Group Baseline Assessment Form.

tion, the occupational therapist may evaluate them using tools such as the Occupational Case Analysis Interview and Rating Scale[1] and Bay Area Functional Performance Evaluation.[2]

Since Directive Group patients don't have the skills required to concentrate on paper-pencil tests, to perform unfamiliar tasks, or to answer interview questions reliably, evaluation methods can't be extensive. Behavioral observation, refined by clinical experience and informed by theory, has been found to be the best instrument.

The initial baseline assessment is based upon observing each patient within the first group session. The co-leaders need to not only observe patients' behavior, but also to associate their responses with the demands of the environment. Throughout the group, the patients are offered opportunities to participate in a series of activities and interactions. The co-leaders must be aware of the capacities required to perform effectively in each aspect of the group. If certain behaviors are not elicited within a group session, then the patients can't be expected to demonstrate evidence of that behavior.

The Baseline Assessment Form (Figure 5-1) provides guidelines for focusing observations and indicating the patient's areas of strengths and weaknesses or function and dysfunction. The behaviors are organized by the volitional, habituation, and performance subsystems and reflect what is considered a basic level for this group. The form is not put into the patient's chart, but the information is summarized in the chart in the S-O-A-P format.[3] Completion of the Baseline Assessment Form is most useful as a training tool for students and co-leaders.

Monitoring Progress

Patient behavior is monitored daily after the group session on the Directive Group Individual Assessment Scale (Table 5-2). The four goals of the group are broken down into a five point rating scale. The descriptors indicate the range of behaviors seen in the group relevant to each goal.

The four outcome goals are listed in the order the co-leaders tend to discuss their observations rather than the hierarchical order of the subsystems as presented in the model of human occupation. *Habits* regarding *attention* to time are rated by how long the patients can focus on the activities of the group. *Communication/Interaction* skills are rated by the amount and quality of verbal *interaction*. *Process and motor* skills are rated by the extent to which patients are able to *participate* in the activities of each session. *Role* behavior is rated by indications of *initiation* through activity ideas (Figure 5-2).

This scale allows for information from the group to be communicated quickly and frequently. The form is posted in the staff room so that any time of day, the staff working with a patient in Directive Group can check on the patient's progress and compare his or her performance with the rest of the group. Weekly summaries of progress are documented in the patient's chart and reported verbally in team meetings. Ideas for modifying this rating scale are discussed in chapter 9.

Documenting Achievement of Goals

Patients are discharged from the group when they consistently perform on

HABITS - Attention Span

5 - Attentive throughout entire session (45 minutes)
4 - Attends for 15-30 minutes
3 - Attends for 5-15 minutes
2 - Attends for 5 minutes or less
1 - Does not attend, highly distractable

SKILLS - Verbal Interaction

5 - Gives spontaneous and appropriate verbal responses to remarks or comments
4 - Responds verbally to direct questioning and is appropriate
3 - Responds moderately to direct questioning (or monopolizes)
2 - Responds minimally or offers inappropriate responses to direct questioning
1 - Does not respond verbally

SKILLS - Participation (Process and Motor)

5 - Cooperates actively in all group activities without assistance
4 - Needs minimal assistance to cooperate actively in group activities
3 - Needs consistent support and structure to assure involvement in activities (or demonstrates hyperactive involvement)
2 - Participates minimally
1 - Uncooperative or resistive towards involvement in group activities

ROLE - Initiation

5 - Suggests, explains, or demonstrates at least one group activity (spontaneous initiation)
4 - Makes suggestions (but may be inappropriate)
3 - Elaborates upon activity ideas with direct assistance
2 - Can choose between two alternatives
1 - Unable to volunteer activities on own

Adapted from The George Washington University Medical Center Inpatient Unit, 1983.

Table 5-2. Directive Group Individual Assessment Scale.

Name		Monday				Tuesday				Wednesday				Thursday				Friday			
Directive Group Progress Sheet Week of _____		Attention Span	Interaction	Participation	Initiation	Attention Span	Interaction	Participation	Initiation	Attention Span	Interaction	Participation	Initiation	Attention Span	Interaction	Participation	Initiation	Attention Span	Interaction	Participation	Initiation

Adapted from The George Washington University Medical Center Inpatient Unit, 1983.

Figure 5-2. Directive Group Progress Sheet.

the upper end (fours and fives) of the rating scale on each of the four outcome goals. Progress and discharge planning is documented in each patient's chart. Transition from the group is handled in consultation with the patient's team and requires the clinical judgment of the co-leaders.

Case Example

Robert's involvement in Directive Group provides an example of how the baseline assessment, rating scale, and progress note forms are used. He also offers a view of how a more active patient is dealt with in a group of predominantly passive members.

Robert, a 25 year old, single, computer technician, was referred to Directive Group because he was negativistic and had poor interaction skills. His primary nurse checked the following specific behaviors on the referral form: inappropriately responds to comments from others; monopolizes interactions despite repeated feedback; and competitive, hyperactive involvement in activities with others. He could get dressed and follow a daily schedule. Nothing was checked about cognitive and task skills, although he had a history of not working as a computer technician for one year prior to admission. He stayed home, fearful and suspicious. He was diagnosed paranoid schizophrenic (Figure 5-3).

When he first attended Directive Group, it was clear he had problems focusing on tasks for five minutes and completing simple activities without assistance. He also made many comments unrelated to the group activities and gave angry, defiant response to comments from others (Figure 5-4). His strengths and weaknesses were documented in the medical record chart. The plan was to participate in the activities and interactions of Directive Group five times a week for at least one week to increase his attention span from about 5 to 10 minutes, increase his ability to interact appropriately, and decrease his hyperactive involvement.

Within the group he was given the goal to focus on the activities of each session. This gave him a channel for his energy and avoided a premature confrontation about his interaction style. He was given support and feedback for his appropriate involvement in activities.

Since most of the members of the group lacked energy, he was next asked to lead exercises, but slowly so that all could participate. This approach helped him to decrease his activity level, notice others, and be aware of their response to him. It also helped the group not get as overwhelmed by his excessiveness and not use him as a scapegoat — as he was viewed during community meetings and informally on the unit.

As his ability to exert internal control improved, he was able to tolerate the more challenging goal of making one comment at a time so that others would have a chance to speak (Figure 5-5). He responded to limits from the co-leaders at times with arguments, but continued to demonstrate eagerness to attend group where he was able to practice self regulation regarding his goals. As he felt safer, his paranoia decreased, and his cognitive and task skills were used to build on his strengths. By the time he left the group, after about two and a half weeks, he was able to state opinions more concisely, take turns

DIRECTIVE GROUP REFERRAL
(Designed to Develop Adaptive Behavior and Basic Skills)

Recent History: Work _Computer tech._

Leisure _____?_____   _Robert_

Relationships ____Ø____   _____
                                              Addressograph

CIRCLE RELEVANT PROBLEM(S) FOR THIS PATIENT SPECIFIED ON MASTER
PROBLEM LIST

___ Disorientation, concrete thinking, decreased concentration
___ Dependent on ADL, passive, helpless
_3_ Social withdrawal, negativistic, (poor interactional skills)
___ Other _____

CHECK SPECIFIC AREAS OF DIFFICULTY FOR THIS PATIENT

Inability to enact roles with others around a common task

___ rarely initiates verbal interactions with others
___ acts aggressively towards others with minimal provocation
_✓_ infrequently or <u>inappropriately</u> responds to comments from others
_✓_ monopolizes interactions despite repeated feedback
___ passive, slowed involvement in activities with others
_✓_ competitive, hyperactive involvement in activities with others

Inability to perform basic self maintenance habits

___ consistently needs assistance to dress self appropriately in a.m.
___ consistently needs assistance to follow daily time schedule

Inability to utilize basic cognitive and task skills

___ inability to focus on single task for more than 5 minutes
___ inability to plan and carry out a simple task without assistance
    (e.g., a familiar, 1-2 step process, e.g., finding meal tray)

Additional information about this patient relevant to participation Directive
Group: _Stayed home past year, fearful and suspicious._

_____

Goals of referral: _Improve ability to interact with others._

_____

Staff Signature _____   Date _____

Figure 5-3. Directive Group Referral Form — Robert.

more easily, and participate in activities with a more even level of energy. See Table 5-3 (p. 56) to compare his initial and final progress ratings from the Individual Assessment Scale.

Just because Robert met the goals of Directive Group, does not mean he is cured or in no need of other types of treatment. In fact, it is more accurate to say that now the work of the more usual therapies could begin, such as, verbal psychotherapy and group therapy, task oriented occupational therapy groups, participating in the recreation program, and collaboration in goal setting and discharge planning. What he developed was a basic level of competence. By the time he was discharged from the hospital about two weeks later, he had returned to his level of functioning prior to needing admission and continued to exceed that level during his follow-up care.

DIRECTIVE GROUP
Baseline Assessment Form

Referral problem(s): # 3   *Poor interaction skills*
S- (What patient said, characteristic statement)
   "Why are you asking me to do that?"
O- PLEASE INDICATE APPROPRIATE RATINGS AND DESCRIPTIONS OF PATIENT'S BEHAVIOR:

Basic Components of Volitional Subsystem	No	Partially	Yes	Not Observed
o Patient identifies personal interests	(1)	2	3	X
o Patient demonstrates goal-directed behavior	1	(2)	3	X
o Patient demonstrates evidence of pleasure in activities, spontaneity, and anticipation of success.	(1)	2	3	X

Comments: (e.g. interests, goals, and motivation)
   Gets involved in each activity, although needs limits to control behavior

Basic Role Behaviors

	No	Partially	Yes	Not Observed
o Patient participates actively in each activity	1	(2)	3	X
o Patient initiates one task related comment/or makes one comment at a time	(1)	2	3	X
o Patient helps lead an activity	(1)	2	3	X

Comments: (e.g. manner/content of interaction, affect and coping skills)
   Monopolizes, suspicious, quick to anger, hyperactive involvement

Basic Self-Maintenance Habits

	No	Partially	Yes	Not Observed
o Patient is dressed in street clothes prior to beginning of session	1	2	(3)	X
o Patient attends group on time	1	2	(3)	X

Comments: (e.g. appearance, response to time expectations)
   Clean, neat, and punctual

Basic Cognitive Skills

	No	Partially	Yes	Not Observed
o Patient is able to stay in session for duration of group	1	2	(3)	X
o Patient is able to focus attention for at least 25 minutes	(1)	2	3	X
o Patient is able to follow instructions on simple tasks	1	(2)	3	X
o Patient is able to explain directions	1	(2)	3	X

Comments: (e.g. fine, gross, and perceptual motor skills, elaborate on cognitive skills)
F, G, & motor skills appear within normal limits. Attention span interferes with task completion.

A- Assess patient's adaptive and maladaptive responses, areas of basic competence, comparison of current performance with past history, environmental requirements necessary to elicit adequate occupational behavior at this level. *Strengths: appearance and punctuality. Can imitate movements and participate in physically oriented activities with structure. Needs firm limits and support to ↑ interpersonal skills. Is responsive to group approach.*

P- Participate in the activities and relationships of Directive group for at least one week to work on the following short-term goal(s):

   1.) Increase attention from 5 to 10 minutes during activities of grp.
   2.) Increase ability to interact appropriately during each group.
   3.) Decrease hyperactive involvement.

   Signature and Discipline's Initials

Figure 5-4. Directive Group Baseline Assessment Form — Robert.

┌───┐

Addressograph

#3   Poor interaction skills

S - "My turn – hurry up. Let's play racquet ball. Why not?"

O - Pt. has attended Directive Group consistently for 8 sessions.
Participates quickly and forcefully in activities. Continues
to monopolize, but responds to support and structure.
attention span has increased from 5 to 20 minutes.

A - Robert is demonstrating more adaptive behavior and
less suspiciousness in group. His strengths
include interest in activities and basic problem-
solving on cognitive tasks (eg. scoring games).
He still has pressured speech, high energy level,
and difficulties interacting with group members. His
numerous activity suggestions indicate initiative, but are
inappropriate for this group environment.

P - Continue in Directive Group for about 5 more sessions
(1 week) with short-term goal: to make one
comment at a time during sessions (so that others
have a chance to speak and pt. increases self-control
and interaction skills.)

                                Kathy L. Kaplan, MS, OTR/L

Figure 5-5. Directive Group Progress Note — Robert.

References

1. Kaplan, K., Kielhofner, G. (1985). Preliminary Manual for the Occupational Case Analysis Interview and Rating Scale. 1415 North Hartford Street, Arlington, VA 22201.
2. Bloomer, J., Williams, S. (1987). The Bay Area Functional Performance Evaluation. Palo Alto, Ca: Consulting Psychologists Press.
3. Weed, L. (1971). Medical Records, Medical Evaluation, and Patient Care. Chicago: Year Book Medical Publishers.

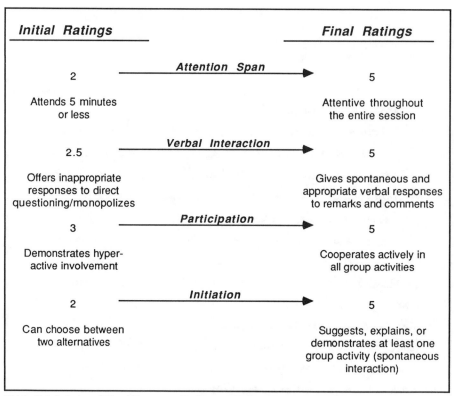

Table 5-3. Inital and Final Progress Ratings — Robert.

Suggested Reading

Hemphill, B. (1982). The Evaluative Process in Psychiatric Occupational Therapy. Thorofare, New Jersey: SLACK.

Kaplan, K. (1982). Inservice Education. Mental Health Special Interest Section Newsletter 5:1 & 3.

Kaplan, K. (1984). Short-term assessment: The need and a response. Occupational Therapy in Mental Health 4 (3) (pp. 29-45).

Kiresuk, T., & Sherman, R. (1968). Goal attainment scoring: A general method for evaluating community mental health programs. Community Mental Health Journal 4:443-453.

Lamb, H. (1982). Young adult chronic patients: The new drifters. Hospital and Community Psychiatry 33:465-468.

Rogers, J. & Kielhofner, G. (1985). Treatment planning. In G. Kielhofner (Ed.) A Model of Human Occupation: Theory and Application (pp. 136-146). Baltimore, MD: Williams and Wilkins.

Schwartz, S. & Goldfinger, S. (1981). The new chronic patient: Clinical characteristics of an emerging subgroup. Hospital and Community Psychiatry 32:470-474.

CHAPTER 6

WHY ARE THEY GIVING ME SUCH A HARD TIME?

Individualizing Patient Goals

In Chapter 5 we talked about the overall goals of the group. It is a common practice for treatment groups to have both group and individual goals. Group goals are important for keeping the group as a whole on track and communicating to others what the group is about. Individual goals help make the group experience more relevant to the patient's problems, strengths, and individual development. They also help the patient get more out of the group by making explicit what he or she is working towards each day.

Besides the benefits to the individual patients, individualized goals send an implicit message to the group that each member is valued as an individual. Groups commonly have concerns about belonging, attachment, inclusion, and intimacy as well as differentiation, separation, control, and power[1]. Even though these concerns are usually not expressed articulately in Directive Group, nor dealt with in depth by the leaders, the issues do emerge. These types of issues will be addressed further in Chapter 8 when examining phases of group development. Here we can see how individual goals serve to preserve each member's identity and help each one experience his or her own differences.

Individual goals also support a feeling of being one of the gang, emphasizing group affiliation. Patients, when presented with individual goals, have an opportunity to exert control through simple negotiation and selective implementation. Examples of this are discussed under individual patient goals (number 8) below.

Individual Patient Goals

The ten patient goals listed below address patient needs common to Directive Group. The goals should be professionally printed on a poster board to make them look attractive and emphasize the importance placed on goal setting. We sometimes show the list of goals to the group and introduce them in a general way during the orientation part of the group. They are also frequently referred to during the wrap-up. The individual patient goals are:

1. Participate actively in each activity.
2. Focus on activities in the session.
3. Follow instructions on tasks.
4. Attend on time, dressed in street clothes.
5. Stay in group for the full 45 minutes.
6. Respond to questions.
7. Listen to others.
8. Make one comment on own per group.
9. Explain directions to others.
10. Help lead an activity.

For some patients the goals are arranged in a hierarchy from easiest to hardest. But no patient seems to need all ten goals over the course of time in the group, especially if he or she is admitted for a week or less. Directive Group patients, being the most dysfunctional on the unit, sometimes stay longer than the "average" two or three weeks. Some stay overnight, while others stay as long as six weeks.

The co-leaders use the goals in any order to evoke the behavior that in their clinical judgment will be the most meaningful change for the patient. It should be a behavior that is within the patient's capacity at the moment. It should also be just the nudge needed to get the individual to function at a little higher level. Sometimes there is a spill-over effect; while working on one goal, behavior in other areas improves also.

Individualizing Patient Goals

The leaders individualize the patient goals during the weekly co-leader meeting. This meeting is in addition to the post-group meetings and usually lasts an hour. Each patient is reviewed in terms of his or her initial baseline assessment, progress to date, and past goals. Then, out of the ten goals, the one that seems the most conducive to helping the individual reorganize his or her behavior is selected. It is rephrased or refined to ensure its meaningfulness for the patient.

Patients at this level cannot set goals for themselves, because goal setting relies on a sense of the past, anticipation of the future, and the ability to assess oneself — functions requiring more internal organization than these patients possess. However, Directive Group patients are receptive to the goals when they are presented in a supportive, respectful, and nonauthoritarian manner.

The leaders think through how to present each goal just as they do any activity analysis. It is more important for the leaders to encourage input from the patients during the discussion of weekly goals than it is for the leaders to put excessive energy into finding the one "right" goal. Our experience suggests that patients value the goal-setting process. It's not unusual to hear patients proudly telling their goals to their nurses or to see patients posting them on their room doors.

The goals are handwritten on a large note card for each patient. The leaders may also make a large chart which lists each patient's name and individual goal. Then there are five spaces for the days in which the group meets. When patients have met their goal for the day, they can check the goal off during the daily wrap-up. The leader asks each patient to say their goal and if they met it. Feedback is solicited from the other patients and co-leaders. The goals are revised once a week so that patients have time for repetition of learning and integration of the behavior.

Relating Group to Individual Goals

The ten individual goals listed above are in general related to the four group goals discussed in Chapter 5, as short-term goals are related to objectives. Group goals indicate expected performance by the end of the stay in the group. Individual goals are steps for implementing one of the group goals by working on it each day (Table 6-1). Sometimes the group goal is used for a given individual, such as to attend the group consistently or to participate in each session. Flexibility in meeting needs is the guiding principle. Each individual patient goal will now be discussed in terms of what it means and how it is commonly used.

Participate Actively in Each Activity. Participation is a standard first goal. It says, get involved in what you do. Adequate performance is demonstrated by basic cooperative behavior and some show of investment in the process. Patients who are very passive and slow may do the activities but look as if they are just going through the motions because their minds are somewhere else. Some people do all the activities but are hyperactive in their involvement. They need cueing to monitor their pace and to keep them from taking over. This may be a good goal for someone who is alert but very resistant to the group. In this case, the goal is clearly a minimal expectation, one which nearly every patient can master.

Focus on the Activities in the Session. The second goal is aimed at patients who are highly distracted from hallucinations, paranoid ideation, or organic confusion. Even though you expect them, as you expect everyone, to participate actively in the activities of each session, you should also attempt to get these patients to focus their attention on the activities. The essence of this goal is to increase a patient's attention span.

Follow Instructions on Tasks. The follow instructions goal is geared at cognitive or process skills. Usually after a week, you can observe which persons do not actively follow what is going on, who watch others and imitate or wait for cueing from the co-leaders. This goal asks them to actively think about what they are doing.

It is important for the leaders to remember who has which goal so they can give each patient an opportunity to demonstrate his or her competence

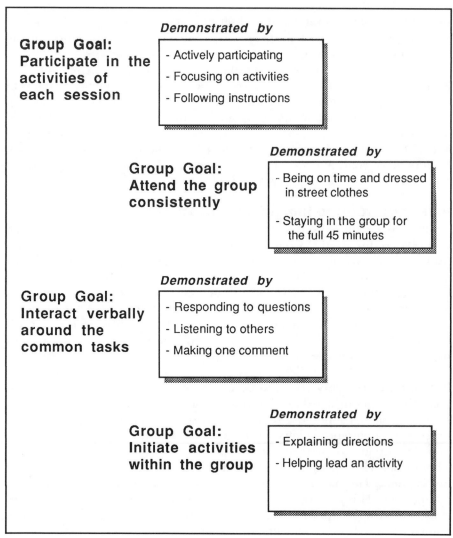

Table 6-1. Relating Group to Individual Patient Goals.

during the group. For instance, if you are going to play a ring toss game, you might ask a particular patient to repeat the instructions after they are explained by the leader. You can make your request not sound like a test question by saying something like, "Jim, would you say for the group the two steps we need to follow to play this game? This will make sure I said them clearly and give you a chance to practice following instructions." Often, you have enough rapport that you don't need to say all that, but you get the idea of how to be soft and supportive.

Attend the Group on Time and Dressed in Street Clothes. To be on time and appropriately dressed is also a general goal for everyone. The kind of people you particularly want to work on this goal are those who are depressed. You and the team feel that staying in pajamas encourages a negative self-image. You need to coordinate with the nursing staff on this goal because they may have to be assigned to the patients before group to assist them in getting dressed. Many patients are disorganized and not attentive to time. This goal is particularly relevant for those patients for whom getting to group on time, again with nursing staff assistance, would be a significant organizing experience.

Stay in Group for the Full 45 Minutes. Everyone is expected to stay the full time, but you will have certain people who can not tolerate this length of time. In fact, in other basic groups, like parallel crafts or exercise, a half hour would probably be a more realistic expectation. Because of the variety this group offers, 45 minutes works well most of the time. The type of person who cannot stay in the group is someone acutely psychotic who is not aware of where he or she is, or is paranoid and not sure it is safe to be in this area. The patient may need to flutter in and out of the room, especially in the first few minutes of the group. Even though this is disturbing to the others, it can be handled very supportively, and behavior usually changes in a few days.

For this person, as he or she start to leave the first time, say something like, "Tammy, we are glad you came to the group. Do you think you could stay for another minute?" If she turns around or looks at you, you have connected and can do business. If she leaves, then she and the group still know she is welcome. If she stays or comes back in, then you can say "We are so glad you are a part of this group. You are welcome to stay as long as you can. Do you think you could stay for five more minutes? Look at the clock. See if you can stay until 9:40."

Once this patient understands that he or she is expected to stay, welcome to stay, and will get support even if he or she can't stay, the patient usually can increase tolerance for the group because you made it feel safe. You are also setting norms for the rest of the group about doing the best you can do. You are giving support, not anger or punitiveness, for an expression of themselves, even if the behavior is distracting for a minute. Of course there are limits. If the behavior continues, you can tell the patient, "This is the last time you can leave for today. You can come back tomorrow. See you at 9:30." Have a co-leader escort the patient to the nursing station and explain what is happening so the patient can be assisted in maintaining control in his or her room and talking about what he or she is feeling, if that is at all possible.

Why close the door, you may ask? We feel most of the patients need the security of having a special time and place for this group. Closing the door helps them to realize, "Hey, we're a group." It emphasizes who is inside and who is outside. This is useful for staff, too, because it legitimizes the therapy. It is not just fun and games. This is a serious attempt to help patients who are severely dysfunctional. The best way to do that may be through using a playful context which involves fun and games, but it doesn't "just happen." In addition, the closed door helps focus the patients' attention to the group itself. Because they generally have trouble screening out external stimuli, the door provides a secure boundary from the rest of the unit. If you don't have a door, find some other ways to provide boundaries.

Respond to Questions. Response to questions is the lowest level of social skills expected in the group. Keep in mind, a patient may be expected to just participate in the activities and never talk (individual patient goal 1); he or he can have nonverbal involvement and be considered successful. But if you feel the patient is ready and able to interact verbally, then responding to a question seems the easiest thing to do.

Here is where offering choices throughout the group gives you many opportunities to let more withdrawn patients react. Also, many of the games require naming names or letters or words, so they automatically talk without realizing it. The wrap-up is also a good time to ask questions which are easy to respond to. For example, "Do you feel as GOOD as you did when you first came to the group this morning, do you feel BETTER than you did at first, or do you feel the BEST you have felt yet? Ronnie, how do you feel, good, better, or best?"

Listen to Others. Listeing to others is a diplomatic approach to aggressive or competitive individuals who tend to monopolize. Another rendition is to ask them to "say one comment at a time, so everyone has a chance to speak." Most people want to be accepted and liked. These types of patients don't mean to be obnoxious to others — this is just how their symptoms are taking expression. If you can give them a way to save face and to learn to control themselves, they are generally appreciative.

All of us do the best we can do most of the time. When we don't seem to be doing well by others' standards, it is probably because unconscious issues and other stresses are preventing more integrated behavior. If you can find within yourself not to assume the person who is being annoying is intentionally being annoying, you will find a supportive response more forthcoming. This often depends on your level of stress and pressing issues, too. It is important not to let your impatience get communicated to the patients. They are extremely sensitive to a perceived slight, punitive response, or condescending attitude.

Make One Comment on Own Per Group. The eighth goal is geared to the person who is generally isolated and needs encouragement to speak up. One comment per group is a measurable goal and is relatively easy to fulfill. The way in which we adapt the goal is to specify the type of comment expected. For instance, one adolescent young man was negative about every activity. His goal was to say one negative comment during the wrap-up. This approach let him feel accepted on the one hand and in control on the other. If he said a negative comment each day, that would show compliance. If he continued the power struggle over the goal and said a positive comment, so much the better. After a few days he started to make constructive comments and demonstrated initiative. He was then receptive to the goal of making one suggestion for an activity each session.

This type of change strategy which turns a problem on its head is characteristic of techniques used by some family therapists. Paradoxical intention and other second-order change strategies have beneficial applications to Directive Group.[2,3] For example, a woman with bipolar depression, depressed phase, refused to respond to the activities. She even let the balloon bounce off of her. Rather than give her attention for trying to gain personal control by this behavior, her goal was to attend the group consistently five days in a row. This allowed her to feel cared about even with her negative attitude, and she was successful because the nursing staff was happy to assist her in attending group.

Her next goal was to do the activities of the session, but "as little as possible." Again, giving her control in this way gave her the choice of either doing more than was expected of her and demonstrating her belief in herself, or actually monitoring how much activity she did. In either scenario she became more involved with the group and her environment and evidenced less depression and resistance.

Explain Directions to Others. Explaining to others is an integrative skill requiring verbal and cognitive skills. This goal is a structured way to begin to show leadership. When a familiar activity is being introduced, the leader asks this patient if he or she would like to explain the directions to the group. If necessary, cueing is provided to keep the explanation simple. This goal helps the patient to make the transition to other groups on the unit which expect some basic leadership ability.

Help Lead an Activity. Leadership is the most complex expectation of a patient in Directive Group. This entails giving directions, answering questions, and helping everyone get set up physically in the room. A few patients request this goal before leaving the group. They are still given support and assistance from the leaders if needed.

Relating Goals to the Treatment Plan

Patients are evaluated daily by a rating scale keyed to the four group goals. How these can be used for program evaluation is discussed in Chapter 9. The important point here is that the patient uses the individual goals to help meet the overall goals of the group.

In the usual scenario patients attend the group one to two weeks. They have reorganized their behavior such that they are able to function at a basic level of competence and are referred to other groups on the unit which meet their further needs. If a patient has no time left in the hospital, he or she is discharged from the group to home with follow-up treatment as determined by the team.

These patients are given a graduation award on their last day in the group. These ribbons or decorative paper state that the patient has met his or her goals in Directive Group from the date of referral until the current date. Handled with dignity by the leaders, the patients seem to enjoy the public recognition of their accomplishment. They provide inspiration for the remaining patients in the group and acknowledge the work done in the Directive Group for other patients outside the group.

A patient who makes no changes in his or her behavior for several weeks, even when various goals have been attempted, may also be discharged from the group. He or she may be discharged to home or, if still in the hospital, have the treatment plan revised. The team and co-leaders try to assess why the patient plateaued, what would be a more helpful approach, and how to implement the other options.

The patient is asked to leave the group, in consultation with the team, because the lack of progress is counterproductive to the patient and the group's morale. The patient may feel bad about not "graduating," but there are many reasons why the person may not be changing at a certain time. Whatever the reasons, the patient is given a disservice if the reality of the situation is not acknowledged. To save face, the patient is allowed to be readmitted to the group after a reassessment at a prearranged date. At the time of leaving the group, the patient's initial substantial gains are recognized and he or she is given a certificate of participation.

Case Example — Sarah

Sarah was a 70-year-old woman with a diagnosis of depression who was being evaluated for organic brain syndrome. Her initial group goal was to attend the group consistently. After two weeks, she was on time for group and dressed in street clothes each day with the help of nursing staff. Her next goal was to participate actively in the activities of each session. However, she participated in the activities of the group slowly and needed consistent support and structure to ensure involvement.

Observations made during group and recorded on the rating scale indicated Sarah attended to activities for 5 to 15 minutes at a time. She needed maximum assistance to follow one-step instructions because her memory and judgment were poor. She did not respond verbally to direct questions and only at times did she use words when required to during games. She never indicated any initiative, not even choosing nonverbally between two activity alternatives.

She was able to remain in the hospital for a relatively lengthy time because her family was able to supplement reimbursement for hospital costs. After two more weeks in the group without responding to individual goals to participate actively or respond to questions, and after much effort to engage her in the treatment process, she was discharged from the group with a certificate of participation. She continued in another group organized at the exploration level of arousal, the exercise group. She was more successful in this group because it was shorter, had less variety of tasks, and was larger so her minimal responses did not affect the morale of the group. This continued to give her the movement and interpersonal stimulation she needed.

She was also seen for individual occupational therapy to work on basic cognitive skills through craft projects. In this environment she was able to make choices about her interests, and she was more successful at interacting than she was in Directive Group. Results of neuropsychologic testing revealed adaptive functioning similar to that found in patients suffering from a progressive degenerative disease, such as Alzheimers or Picks. Since she would be discharged to a nursing home to provide the substantial supervision she required, the individual craft had meaning to her and would perhaps make it easier for her to interact with others over time. In addition, the individual sessions gave her a highly structured, familiar, and simplified environment with adequate supervision. While most of the patients on the ward have an acute condition for which they relatively quickly recompensate, some patients, like Sarah, seem to have a longer term illness which is more responsive to slower paced expectations for change.

References

1. Bennis, W., Sheppard, H. (1974). A theory of group development. In Gibbard. G., Hartman, J., Mann, R. (Eds.). Analysis of Groups. San Francisco: Jossey Bass, pp.127-153.
2. Haley, J. (1978). Problem-Solving Therapy: New Strategies for Effective Family Therapy. (pp. 67-76). San Francisco: Jossey-Bass.
3. Watzlawick, P. (1978). The Language of Change. New York: Basic Books.

Suggested Reading

Mager, R. (1972). Goal Analysis. Belmont, CA: Fearon.
Mager, R., Pipe, P. (1971). Analyzing Performance Problems or "You Really Oughta Wanna." Belmont, CA: Fearon.

CHAPTER 7

WHAT DO I DO NOW?
Leading the Group

The most important focus for the Directive Group is to provide direction for the patients. How do the leaders do this without being overly directive? There are several key ways that the leaders can best help the patients become more self-directed: through being a role model for action, support, and interaction; by creating a playful context; by offering choices; and by organizing the space.

Who Leads the Group?

The first item of business is to discuss who leads this group. We always talk about leaders, plural, because the group can't do what it needs to do with only one person's energy. This group is geared towards people who are largely nonfunctional. They may be acutely psychotic, very depressed, or chronically ill with limited skills for thinking, doing, and talking. So, how do you create an atmosphere for healthy, playful interaction when you only have yourself to rely on? You'll end up burned-out from using up your own steam or seem silly to the patients because you are out there all alone. You need consensual validation from other well-balanced adult leaders. You need the support and interplay of at least one other person who understands the context in which you are operating.

Because the patients are so disorganized, it is essential the group meet routinely. Co-leadership ensures continuity of the group during staff vacations or illness. Co-leaders also provide security when a patient requires individual attention or assistance to leave the room because of out-of-control behavior. And what happens when you get overwhelmed? Sometimes the group dynamics exert a powerful pull toward passivity or disruptiveness. You may not have the energy to turn things around all on your own. Don't kid yourself, this group is demanding. You have to plan lots of activities every day it meets. There are lots of goals to set and progress notes to write. Have I made the argument clear? You need co-leaders!

Okay, I know there are practical limitations on staff time. But there are ways to get co-leaders if you are willing to have a little patience, ingenuity, and flexibility (more about this in Chapter 9). The important point is to get some staff or student support. Look to nursing staff, psychiatric technicians, social workers and psychologists, other activity-oriented personnel, medical students on rotation, occupational therapy interns, and even the psychiatrists. With at least one other person, even if that co-leader alternates with others, you can create the type of environment necessary to conduct a Directive Group.

Being a Role Model

You can't lead Directive Group by nodding your head and saying, "Can you say more?" You have to be right out there — vulnerable, active, and maybe even more yourself than usual. Why? Because you are working with patients who are very fragile emotionally. They have extreme anxiety that manifests itself in many behavior patterns: action paralysis, hyperactivity, withdrawal, negativity, whatever. They need someone strong to identify with and come up against. They need to know where they start by knowing where you end. So you have to provide boundaries for them. And you do this through the structuring of the room, the activities, and your interactions.

The co-leaders need to develop a relationship with each other in which they feel very supported. You can look at each other and know it's time to change the activity, or step in and help explain instructions, or switch gears altogether. You have to fill in the various group membership roles that make for effective groups. You encourage, cajole, refocus, challenge, suggest, or do anything else you think is needed. This type of flexibility rubs off on the patients. They can sense your rapport and feel supported by it.

As you participate in the activities of each session, you provide role models for action. You show that you value meaningful activity. You also show that you value relationships by the caring you give to each member.

You keep the interactions on a rather task-oriented level because sharing intimate feelings or personalized delusions is too overwhelming for these patients. You can tease each other, but be careful about teasing patients. They interpret words very concretely and can feel extremely criticized by sarcasm. What you want is to let your benign sense of humor find expression, but not by putting anyone down or casting situations in a negative light. You need to focus your energy on giving patients lots of feedback about their behavior. You are putting into words the effects of their actions so that they can recognize that they do have control and competence. You are their reality check; you are continuously providing validation that "Yes, this is really happening."

Most of all, the best gift you offer the patients is acceptance. You say to them through your actions and words that they are valuable human beings. You expect each of them, when they are ready, will be successful, and you will support them in all attempts to participate. When they begin to internalize that self-acceptance, they can begin to truly change.

Creating a Playful Context

The way to be a role model is first to understand the context you are attempting to create. The group is organized at the exploration level because you are trying to help patients develop basic skills. The patients at this level need a context in which they can feel accepted, experience success, and begin to focus on life outside of themselves. Psychosis is such a devastating experience, that, as one of the psychiatric faculty once said, it is akin to getting hit by a truck. It is easy to imagine how much that hurts and how long it would take to recover. So now, you can see why it is so hard for these patients to want to master and explore their world. They have lost that urge because they are dealing on a survival level. Your role is to help these people feel safe, start to heal, and gradually get back to the business of productive living.

One way to do this is through the context of play. Some of you may associate play with being a child and summer camp. Well, that is normally when play is the major activity of life, just as school occupies the adolescent years, and work is the focus of adulthood. But during adulthood, one developmental task is to have balance in life from multiple, often conflicting, roles. In this way play, thought of as leisure time and recreational activities, provides an outlet for fun, spontaneity, and relaxation. Often it is an arena for creative expression or for developing skills not used in work or during caretaking responsibilities.

However, this is the play of the fairly emotionally well balanced adult. For the extremely disorganized, very disturbed patient, we are after a different conceptualization of play. We are trying to create the basic components that are evident in adult play, but at a less conceptual and integrated level. Components of play include elements such as feeling okay about making mistakes because the point is to enjoy yourself and the company of others; acting silly or laughing a lot because the focus is on having fun and not carrying out a responsible role, like a job; not having to be good at everything because part of the incentive of play is to try something new and see what happens or what it is like.

If you are going to create the context of play for these patients, then you need to act in such a way that they feel safe to make mistakes, can begin to enjoy the process, and not feel achievement pressure and performance anxiety. How do you do that? First, by feeling that way yourself. You can throw the ball and miss the target and still be a good person. Second, by structuring activities so the emphasis is on the process and not the product. Winning and losing is secondary to seeing how long the group can keep the balloon in the air. Third, by changing the activity on the spot if it is too challenging, so that patients do not get too anxious; for instance, changing to a group score for modified bowling so the emphasis is not on individual success or failure.

Granted, the playful context evokes memories of childhood, especially when you have adults who know on some level that they cannot handle very complex activities, but also realize that they are adults, after all. Being sensitive to their divided selves, their past experiences in contrast with their current functional abilities, is one of the greatest challenges of the therapist role. Somehow you must convey respect for these individuals no matter how dysfunctional they currently are, and be careful not to talk down to them, act patronizing, or inadvertently make fun of them. At the same time, you must convey the feeling that play is definitely a legitimate way for adults to interact at times.

If the patients say the game seems childish, you have lots of options. You can acknowledge that it is often hard to play, for them and yourself. If you as a leaders have reservations about using these types of activitites, you'll have to confront your own discomfort and ultimately decide if the group is for you. If you can work with your mixed feelings, you can reassure them that it is okay for adults to play basic games and to enjoy themselves. You can ask the patients if they would like to change the game to make it more adult and fun for them, or if they would rather do a different activity. You can explore why they feel it's childish, if you think they can express their concerns. You can ask them when was the last time they played games. Or you can ask them what they like to do for fun and relaxation. The important point is to try to discover what the comment means to them at this moment and respond in the most helpful, nonthreatening way. What you don't want to do is become defensive about the rightness of your approach or deny or put down their experience of the activity. The issue is not really the specific activity or method. Patients in verbal group therapy as well often wonder if talking really helps. The issue is respect for patients' process and perception of the group and relationships as truly helpful to them.

Offering Choices

One of the factors that greatly counteracts the patients' reaction (i.e., demeaned, insulted) to basic activities they feel are childish is offering choices. When patients are offered choices, they recognize that their contributions are valued and that they are necessary in shaping the form the group takes. The control they exert is real, even if limited. As a leader, you must never take their influence for granted and usurp decision-making on such "little things."

Like an activity analysis, the choices must be offered in a graded approach. Think of a series of concentric circles. Now imagine that they are glass lenses which can be held up to the eyes to see the world, as if looking through a telescope. If you focus on the smallest, central circle, you can only see things right in front of you. If you open the aperture to the next largest circle, incorporating the one inside it, you can focus on more of the world at a little farther distance. The next level allows you to see clearly a much larger area, changing your sense of the environment which is in front of you.

Offering choices is like controlling the aperture on the lens. You structure the world of choices based on what each patient can tolerate. For instance, the smallest level might be deciding between two ways to do an activity. "Do you want to play dodge ball (by rolling a Nerf ball at the person's feet in the center of a circle) sitting or standing?" Since you can play the game either way, the choice is safe because it doesn't matter. It is clearly a matter of preference, probably based on energy level, which is best ascertained by the participant.

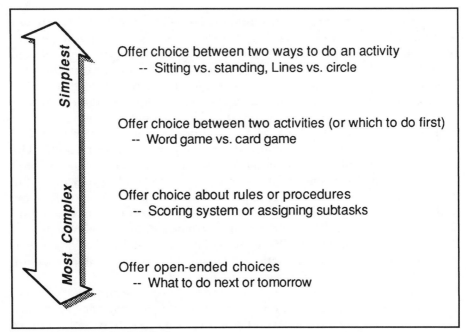

Table 7-1. Offering Graded Choices.

A similar type of question is whether to play the game in two lines (teams) or a circle. The patients can usually tell you where their investment is for that moment, in cooperating with the whole group or competing between two subgroups (Table 7-1).

The next level might be to decide between two activities: would they rather play one game or another? Maybe you think they could handle either a word game, like matching the alphabet on the blackboard to geography, or a card game, like playing Uno around a table. They can decide which one, or if both, in what sequence.

A more complex level would be to have the group decide on the rules for a game or the procedures for an activity. For instance, they could make up a system for keeping score of balloon volleyball or modified bowling. Or they could decide who should do which task when coloring the numbers for a monthly calendar.

Finally, you could offer an open-ended choice about what to do based on their past interests. Some patients who are getting ready to graduate from the group are even able to help lead the activity. You can ask an experienced group member what activity he or she would like to do next or for the main activity tomorrow. Don't ask for ideas unless you are ready to give them control and are prepared to follow through on their suggestion. If you can't do the activity right then, be prepared to explain why.

Organizing Space

A few words are needed about the physical environment. Everyone is affected by their surroundings, some more than others. Psychotic patients tend toward the extremes, as you might expect: oblivious (when preoccupied with hallucinations or experiencing overwhelming depression) or hypersensitive (when preoccupied with paranoid thoughts or experiencing loose ego boundaries). Whatever your own preferences are in your surroundings for neatness, order, and pleasantness, you need to attend to these features of the environment for the sake of the patients. You can influence their degree of internal organization by how you organize the external environment.

The room you use should be relatively clutter-free, but not sterile looking. Posters, calendars, or projects made by the group can decorate the walls. The objects you use should be functional and provide cues to the patients about what to expect. For instance, chairs placed in a circle when they enter the room convey a message to sit. A paper on the door listing everyone's name and the days of the week with a pen hanging on a string suggests it is expected that patients check off their names upon coming to group (although they may need assistance to do this task routinely). An easy-to-read clock emphasizes the importance of the patients staying oriented to time and pacing themselves until the group session ends.

As leader, you need to have an eye on the space you use and how you fill it. If the group has few patients, you can make the room seem smaller by how you arrange the tables or chairs. If you are trying to convey a cooperative attitude, then be sure the physical arrangement of the room does not inadvertently suggest teams and competition. The little things, such as having all the pieces of a game intact, having extra balloons ready in case one pops, or having supplies and equipment that look appealing, all reinforce the message you are trying to give about valuing the patients and the shared group experience.

Theoretical Underpinnings

According to the model of human occupation, the context of play is appropriate for generating basic skills at the exploratory level. Skills are essential to develop in Directive Group patients because their lack of skill severely constrains the rest of their open system functioning. With healthy, functioning adults, when they want to learn a new skill, such as tennis or photography, the most facilitative framework is one in which there are few pressures to perform. There should be time to get to know the equipment, take shots without penalty for mistakes, and just enjoy the process of learning. Directive Group is organized at this exploratory level to rekindle patients' interest in the world around them.

Offering choices and giving patients a realistic sense of reestablishing control is an aspect of building personal causation. This component is part of the volitional subsystem. As the highest level of the throughput hierarchy, it commands the habituation and performance subsystems. Therefore, in treatment it is important to engage this level to help the patients exert choice over developing the lower levels.

In helping patients reverse their maladaptive cycle and aim for a self-enhancing path of development, the environment has a large influence. The patients bring with them expectations and values based on their home environments. Then the hospital and group setting create a different environment for developing occupational behavior. The group leaders need to be sensitive to individual/environment interactions and create an environment that is compatible with the patients' culture, lifestyle, and abilities.

Suggested Reading

Bateson, G. (1955). A theory of play and fantasy. Psychiatric Research Reports (2), 39-51.

Bruner, J. (1976). Nature and Uses of Immaturity. Play: Its Role in Development and Evolution. New York: Basic Books.

Kielhofner, G. (1983). The art of occupational therapy. In Kielhofner, G. (Ed.): Health Through Occupation. Philadelphia: F.A. Davis, pp.295-309.

Reilly, M. (Ed.). (1974). Play as Exploratory Learning. Beverly Hills, CA: Sage.

Vandenberg, B., Kielhofner, G. (1982). Play in evolution, culture, and individual adaptation: Implications for therapy. Am J Occup Ther 36(1):20-28.

CHAPTER 8

EVERYONE'S SO DIFFERENT
Adapting Activities

Can you learn to be creative and intuitive? I think so, I practiced by teaching a predominately "left-brained"[1] friend — who follows recipes step-by-step as if they were strict rules — how to plan meals and adapt recipes more creatively. Those of us who are more "right-brained" than rational, have spent years learning how to be more logical, sequential, and systematic. Most self-help manuals are based on such techniques. Now it's time to incorporate both sides of the brain through leading Directive Group.

I'm going to attempt to make explicit how I get the feel of a group and adapt my plans on-the-spot. Creativity and intuition are necessary functions of the effective group leader. I believe everyone has the capacity to use them, but some people get more practice than others. If these modes come easy for you, you probably tend to use them whenever you have a chance in your daily activities.

If these modes are not your preference, then be gentle with yourself when learning these new skills. At first, you won't feel comfortable and you won't trust your judgment based on an "intuitive feel." I suggest you let go of your critical inner voice for the moment and take a risk. Reflect on the process and make rational alterations later.

Also, don't attempt to compartmentalize the information which follows. Part of fostering your creative and intuitive self depends on perceiving the gestalt of things, getting the whole picture, seeing the lay of the land. Just let the ideas exist simultaneously. Analyzing them, evaluating their consistency, and drawing conclusions are rational functions which you already know how to use well (that's why you keep wanting to bring them into this unfamiliar arena) and will interfere with the use of your processing functions.

Getting a Feel for the Group

Even though each patient in Directive Group is an individual, when they are assembled together the unit of analysis is a group. Think of the group as an entity. Now, how can you get to know this entity? — by being receptive to the energy level, degree of interaction, and amount of initiative and responsiveness which is being expressed.

Let's take an example. Sometimes you walk into the room when it is time for the group to meet and only a few patients are there. The rest come straggling in one at a time. Eyes are riveted to the floor or staring into space. There is very little conversation. No one looks at you or asks any questions. You start to feel a weight within yourself, pulling you down. You wonder why, when only minutes before you were busily preparing for the group; now you suddenly feel tired. You wonder if any of your planned activities will be appropriate.

The questions you ask yourself and the feelings you notice within yourself are indicators of group needs. They also indicate your sensitivity to the group and yourself. Rather than feel discouraged about the group's effect on you, recognize that you are using your empathic capacity and self-awareness.

Now let's look at how you perceived the group's needs. First you noticed their energy level, although you may not have described it as such. The patients did not move quickly, appear to engage in activity, or speak very much. The overall slowness, detachment, and lack of involvement were signals of a group with low energy. Then, the amount of conversation and listening behavior observed among the members gave you an indication of the degree of interaction. Most of the members were not talking to each other. Even if two patients came in already engaged in conversation, it was of few words and little animation. No one else looked at them speaking to show a desire to contribute to the conversation. The interaction level was low.

The levels of initiative and responsiveness were also low. At the beginning of the group, initiative is demonstrated by someone offering a suggestion or making a move to get the group started. Responsiveness is demonstrated by someone readily reacting to the suggestion or joining in the effort to begin the activity. In the above example, no one demonstrated initiative and there was little indication of responsiveness. Lack of eye contact with the leaders suggested a lack of anticipation of action. However, the fact the patients were entering the room and staying in it let you know there was some willingness to be engaged.

Phases of Group Development

With closed groups, such as the outpatient groups discussed in Chapter 1, there are predictable developmental stages that generally occur over the course of the group meetings. These have been referred to as forming, storming, norming, and performing.[2] Each phase brings out different issues. When the group is first forming, individuals' insecurities about what to expect in a new situation often cause them to inhibit themselves while gathering data about their first impressions.

Once the group has tested the boundaries a little, the group's dependency issues turn to concern for power and control. During the storming phase, the leader is often criticized and members try to exert influence. At some point, the alliances formed during the second phase get redrawn. The pointlessness of continuing the hostility is aired and members try to create norms for harmony and build cohesion.

The performing phase results from the group looking over its development and trying to not only maintain the structure and goodwill of the norming phase, but also be honest with each other about how to meet emotional needs at the same time as task goals. The effective group develops functional role relationships and shared responsibility before preparing for ending the group.

Four Types of Directive Group Sessions

Directive Group is an open group in that patients constantly come and go and there are no set number of sessions all will attend together. Therefore, the phases of group development aren't as sequential as in a closed group. Yet, over the years, we have found a pattern of four different types of Directive Group sessions which frequently recur. They are the *immobilized group*, the *negativistic passivity group*, the *prototypic Directive Group*, and the *parts to the whole group*. Each type appears to be influenced by the patient composition, group cohesiveness, and ward issues external to the group. However, none of these factors has been traced in any predictable way to what occurs in the group. I've been confronted with an immobilized group at the beginning of the week, when there are new members, after a special community meeting, and following an active group the preceding day.

When reflecting on the four types of groups that commonly occur, I was struck by the issues that ran parallel with the four stages of group development. (Remember, psychiatry is a retrospective science. Once you know what has occurred, you can work backwards to figure out the whys.) While there is no way to be sure of the reasons why certain needs are expressed in the group, the developmental stages provided an interesting way to think about what happens. (Even though the group has been around for a while, there are still many fruitful areas for conceptual development. Clearly, this is one of them.)

The intent of this section is to prepare you for the unexpected by describing what problems we have observed and the solutions we have found effective. The operating principle is "when the task breaks down, deal with the process." Based on hundreds of group sessions, these suggestions offer ways of dealing with the process which we have found to work with for patients at this level. Included are examples of specific activities we have used with each type of group.

The Immobilized Group

The immobilized group seems to have a need to wait. Their issues are similar to the forming stage of group development in that they show extreme inhibition. This group as a whole is characterized by extreme lethargy, quiet, and lack of initiative or response. It's as if the group is waiting for the right thing to move them, but there is little expectation it will happen. So the patients seem content to sit and watch and wait. The leaders are challenged to gear their own energy down to an idle, without getting angry or falling asleep.

What we found brings this type of group around is patience, warmth, and structure from the leaders. The pace starts slow to match the patients' energy level. Most of the activities are movement-oriented with attention to perceptual skills and with few cognitive demands. The activities need to be simple so as not to overchallenge the skill level of the group or to give a sense of being too controlling.

You cannot imagine how slowly you may need to do each activity. You may feel like laughing because the group is so passive it's ridiculous. But you must find it within yourself to be respectful of these needs and match them. We have found the slow exercises, starting with moving one finger, particularly effective. Sometimes the group is able to start laughing at itself when members realize how slow they are moving. Then you know you've broken through the resistance. You'll feel a shift in the tension of the group, and you'll feel they are "with you" and you can adapt from there.

Typical activities for an immobilized group session might include the following:

1. **Welcome each member by name.** Review date (have a person change the arrow on the large calendar or have a person write the date on the blackboard), time of group, and name of group.

2. **Exercise.** Sitting on chairs in a circle, have patients imitate leaders doing movements beginning with one finger. Gradually include whole hand and expand to arms, making faces, and large movements.

3. **Name ball game.** Each person gently throws a large red balloon to one member at a time while calling out that person's name. If someone does not know the person's name, he or she is encouraged to ask.

4. **Sit down soccer.** Sitting in a circle or two lines facing each other, kick a Nerf ball under or between the chairs. Everyone tries to block the ball with his feet.

5. **Bean bag toss.** Throw colored bean bags onto a large mat which has matching colored circles. Members can aim to match the colors, or keep score by assigning each circle a point value.

6. **Wrap-up.** Ask members to state the activities done that day. The leader writes them on the blackboard in order. Ask the patients to raise their hand for the activity they liked the best. Provide positive feedback individually to members.

The Negativistic Passivity Group

A more fiesty type of group is characterized by negativistic passivity. Their issues are similar to the storming stage in that they vie for power and control. Here the patients act as if the leaders are supposed to take the lead, but they keep doing it wrong. So the patients refuse to follow the lead. They may act bored or refuse to participate in some of the activities. No suggestions or alternatives are supported.

What seems to bring this group around is active stimulation. The activities are largely movement-oriented, but have more cognitive and interactive demands than the previous type of group. Plan to include as many activities as possible which require little waiting and are easily completed.

The negativity may be addressed directly in a playful way by stopping whatever you are doing and involving the group in a round of yes and no. You designate half the group as yes's and the other half as no's. Tell each half to yell their word as loud as possible in response to each other. You won't believe what a great tension releaser this is. Again, when you have perceived this need accurately, the patients often laugh at themselves, indicating their resistance has been recognized.

This is largely an unconscious process. Your enabling them to have mixed feelings about the group without punishing them is highly therapeutic. Usually the members' expectations of success and belief in themselves increases noticeably after an experience like this.

Both the immobilized and negativistic passivity groups are passive, but the first is expressed nonverbally and indirectly and the second is expressed in action or words. Each is resisting change and depending on the leaders in an extreme amount. Each group requires the leaders to deal with the emotional blocks before any skill development can occur.

The leaders need to perceive the group process and be willing to respond to the needs expressed in a productive way for this level patient. Insisting on "the plan" will not be therapeutically useful because it denies the reality of what is happening and doesn't release the potential energy of the group, even if it is minimal at best.

The following are typical activities for a negativistic passivity group session:

1. **Begin by introducing new members.** Ask patients to explain what is done in Directive Group and what are the goals of the group.

2. **Name ball game.** Use this activity to provide reinforcement and repetition. Expand from names to other categories, like hobbies or names of states.

3. **Exercise.** Each member leads one movement for the rest to follow. Use getting from sitting in a circle to standing as part of one of the exercises.

4. **Parachute activities.** Sitting first, members begin by making soft waves, adding balls, then standing and changing places by calling out names. These activities involve everyone and can be varied in increasing complexity.

5. **Fruit basket game.** Each person sits in a chair in a circle. There is one less chair than the number of people. Each person is labeled one of three kinds of fruit, like apples, oranges, and pears. The person standing calls out a fruit and people with that label change places. When "fruit basket" is called, everyone changes places.

6. **Velcro darts.** Members stand at a distance which is challenging for them and throw Velcro ping-pong balls at the target. Names are written in order on the blackboard and each person writes his or her own score.

7. **Wrap-up.** The discussion may be a game called Guess What? The leader asks the group questions and writes the responses on the board. For example, What was the best thing about the group today? What was the most fun? What was the slowest game?

The Prototypic Group

The next type of group is the prototypic Directive Group. The group seems to have a need to focus and demonstrates a sense of harmony typical of the norming stage. Here the group acts as if there is potential energy if only it can be directed. The leaders need only to respond by providing structure, a playful context, appropriate activities, supportive relationships, and the other factors typical of Directive Group.

The patients show the beginnings of initiative, longer attention spans, and some spontaneous interaction. The group can focus on a longer activity than the preceding two groups. The leaders can select activities which involve fine motor and interaction challenges. More choices are offered regarding the sequence and selection of activities. The group is structured to capture both personal and group interests.

The following is a sample session for the prototypic group:

1. **Introduction.** Leaders may focus a discussion on punctuality by asking "Who remembered to come to the group on their own? When is it necessary to be on time outside of the hospital?" The purpose of the discussion is to expand attention to time from the present to past and future situations.

2. **Names.** Each member may be given a name tag with someone else's name on it. One at a time they are to give the name tag to the correct person.

3. **Simon Says.** The instructions are reviewed and the game is first led by a co-leader. Then other members lead, using their own names, for example, "Mary says . . . "

4. **The next activity may be a team game, like balloon volleyball or human tic-tac-toe.** Alternatively, the group members may each do an individual craft, like a fabric memo pad. There should be sufficient materials for each person to make his or her own project while passing some of the supplies to others to share. Each person may be asked to show the finished project to the group and say how he or she plans to use it.

5. **If there is a little lag time, start a quick game of modified charades.** Cards are distributed with ideas such as, pretend to be hitting a baseball or pretend you're eating a lemon.

6. **Wrap-up.** Ask members to identify the skills required for performing the activities done today. The patients are surprisingly good at identifying skills and pleased when they realize how many they used during the group.

The Parts to the Whole Group

The fourth type of group we refer to as "parts to the whole" because typically each person carries out a portion of the activity which is then combined at the end. The group seems to have a need to contribute. Their functional role relationships and shared responsibility resemble the characteristics of the performing stage.

This type of group feels like a gift to the leaders when it occurs, it's so rare. In this group, the patients take over some of the leadership functions. They make suggestions, such as making a birthday cake for one member. This is still at a basic skill level of interaction, but the sharing tone and urge to give is new for this type of group.

Often individual members are able to assist in leading portions of the activity or helping those who are less organized to perform. The group reflects a value orientation toward productivity. Patients who are functioning at this level are ready to be in other groups on the unit. The leaders need only to structure the activities so that each can take a role that contributes to the group as a whole. Then you can enjoy the fruits of your labors!

A typical session for the parts to the whole group is as follows:

1. **Introductions.** Sitting in a circle, ask each patient, in sequence, to introduce the person on his or her left to the person on his or her right.

2. **Exercise.** Begin by standing and gradually increase energy and complexity. For example, ask each member to touch and name three body parts in a row while the group repeats the actions.

3. **The selected activity may be a mural divided into sections for each member; a fruit salad with each person cutting a different fruit, assembling it in one bowl, then serving to each person; or a large calendar.** Each month the co-leaders design a large calendar with a theme which matches the month. Supplies are brought in for the patients to outline, cut, and paste large numbers each day. Discussion of special days during the month follows.

4. **There may be a short game at the end emphasizing cognitive skills and encouraging spontaneity.** For example, playing Who Am I? involves one member guessing the name of the animal written on a piece of paper on his or her back by asking yes or no questions. (e.g.,"Am I in the zoo?")

5. **Wrap-up.** Guess Who? Patients discuss who took various roles in the group after the leaders write the questions on the board. For example, who was helpful to others? Who helped lead the activity? Who was very organized? Who was funny?

Optimal Arousal Levels

Even though the above descriptions of the four type of groups will help to prepare you for what to expect when leading Directive Group, your best bet is to count on the group being different from what you expected. The question is what form it will take. To deal with these surprises, your best protection is to be comfortable with the process of adapting activities.

The main concept influencing how to adapt activities, and which is implied in each of the above examples but not fully described, is optimal arousal levels. This means you want a match between the patients' needs and the activities which will meet those needs. It is not dissimilar to the goal in job hunting for yourself. You have certain interests, goals, preferences, and skills related to work. You interview with several potential employers to learn about the position they are trying to fill. Based on a comparison of what each has to offer, you decide to take the job that provides the best opportunity for expressing your professional interests, achieving your career goals, matching your preferences for salary and environment, and developing your particular skills.

Now think about your leisure time and how you go about planning to enjoy a favorite activity. If you like to ski, but don't get a chance to practice very much, you would greatly look forward to your one weekend a year to ski. To refresh your motor memory you might start on the bunny slope and then take a group lesson. After a little refreshment and rest, you are ready for the long easy, intermediate hills. You are excited and progressing nicely. Then you see your friends paralleling down the expert slopes, and they try to convince you to go up the chair lift and ski with them. You are terrified because you perceive, accurately, that they are expecting more from you than you have the ability to perform at this time. So you decline, then your little brother pops up and asks you to take him on the bunny slope so he can learn to snow plow. You don't really want to do it (even though you might acquiesce to be nice or to win points for future favors) because you are past that now. It is boring and would keep you from challenging yourself.

The same ideas apply to Directive Group. You want to provide an environment which is optimally arousing for the patients. If you present an activity which is too taxing, the group will get anxious and not be able to perform well. They will want to leave, interrupt conversation, bring up off-the-wall comments, or just space out. If the demands of the environment are too understimulating, patients will be bored and not perform well. They will want to leave, interrupt conversation, bring up off-the-wall comments, or just space out. Both directions end in the same place.

But when you hit it right, the patients have a little bit of anxiety which is facilitory. They are energized and alert and willing to invest in the process. You have hit the "just right" challenge. I'm not saying they'll be angels, but you will be seeing them function better than they usually do. (I have often used the concept of optimal arousal levels, as portrayed in Figure 8-1, during inservice presentations as an overview to the referral system and graded approach of the group treatment program.)

How Do You Adapt Activities in Planning?

I'm going to think out loud with you to show you the process by which we brainstorm activities for a group and make adaptations as necessary once we see how the group is responding. It is easiest if you start with the segment of the group you want to deal with, be it the warm-up activities, the middle of the group-selected activities, or the wrap-up activities.

Now think about the energy level of the group as a whole and decide how much you want to match it or challenge it by nudging them toward slightly more or less action. Next, think about the individual patients and about how they compare on their skill levels. This will tell you the range of abilities and whether they are all about the same or if one or two of them stand out in some area. Finally, you review the activities at your disposal and see what fits. The Appendix provides a host of activity ideas which may help you expand your resources.

As an example, the group as a whole is rather slow and passive. The individual members do not vary much in their skill areas. You want to think of something that matches their skills and interests for a middle of the group-selected activity. What are their capacities? First, you see that most of the patients can only follow one- or two-step processes. So you try to choose activities that have one or two steps, or can be presented in one- or two-step subunits.

Then you think about their emotional needs. They need an activity that

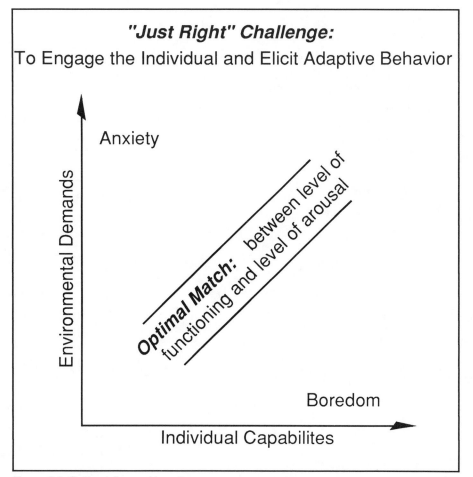

Figure 8-1. Optimal Arousal Levels.
Adapted from Csikszentmihalyi, M. (1975). Beyond Boredom and Anxiety.

has little need for self-awareness and would not make them feel vulnerable to others. So you pick something relatively neutral emotionally.

When you analyze their communication skills, you decide they need to feel comfortable just doing activities in the presence of others, rather than having to carry on an extended conversation at this point. So you set up a parallel group situation.

You also look at their gross, fine, and perceptual-motor skills. You may find you have a low energy group and want to use fine motor skills with basic demands for figure-ground perception.

The next step involves reviewing categories of activities. Do you want a sit-down game or a craft? Do you want to emphasize verbal skills or physical exercise? Do you want to focus attention with an object, like a parachute or balloon, or just rely on moving bodies or stimulating memories? Ask yourself questions and explore alternatives until one feels as if it has potential. You perceive a light going on or sense a shift in yourself which allows you to recognize that the idea matches your criteria (Figure 8-2).

```
GUIDELINES:

1.  Every group takes planning.  Plan based on previous day.

2.  Analyze activities selected for each segment of the group.
    Review the categories of activities and available supplies.

3.  Respond to both the energy level of the group-as-a-whole
    and the variations in performance of the individuals within the group.

4.  Be prepared to grade activities up or down depending on the responses
    of the group members.  Consider needs for novelty, complexity, and
    uncertainty.


SEQUENCE OF EVENTS:

A.  Orientation to group



B.  Introductions of new members, review of names



C.  Warm-up exercises



D.  Selected activities (Consider motor, cognitive, interactive skills,
    and emotional needs)




E.  Wrap-up, individual goals



F.  Post-group (Division of responsibilities, future planning)
```

Figure 8-2. Planning and Adapting Group Session.

Session Example

Let's say you want a craft activity. You remember an issue which was discussed in community meeting and surfacing informally on the ward is that of taking care of each other. Yesterday, in Directive Group during the balloon game when naming hobbies, two people said they liked to garden. You wonder if there is anything thing you can do with plants. How about simple terrariums? You have an overgrown spider plant from which you have been rooting the little spider cuttings in water and haven't decided what to do with them yet. Things start to click in your mind.

You saw terrariums at an art show recently — fish bowls with colored sand on the bottom and dirt and a plant on top. What if you used small plastic cups like those used for drinking at parties or picnics? That size should be manageable for the limited time frame of the group.

Then, in order to not have too many options which would overwhelm patients' cognitive capacities, you could select four or so colors of sand and prepour them into small paper medicine cups. These would be easy to store and for patients to pour. You could show them how to pour a little of one color into the bottom of the cup. Have them do it. Then pour another color. They follow. Then the first color again. Then let them pour any colors until the cup is half full. In this way the process is in small steps.

Then you could give everyone a cup of dirt to place on the top. Then you could give them each a cutting from your overgrown spider plant. With your co-leader and student there to assist individual members, it seems doable. In fact, terrarium plants meets your criteria for the cognitive demands, the low energy level, and the parallel group structure. You would build on their fine motor and perceptual motor skills. And you could titrate the emotional and communication demands based on the response once in the activity. Certainly the terrarium is relatively neutral, but they could express themselves through their individual designs and color selection of sand.

The main issue is that this activity takes a lot of preparation. You decide you have the energy and interest for it, you have most of the supplies on hand, and you can ask your student to help you set up a half-hour before the group.

How Do You Adapt Activities on the Spot?

You get into the group and it is still basically at a low energy level, so you think the selected activity will fly. You do some slow warm-ups and exercises and then move to the table for the bulk of the time left. One member is a little distracted while you are setting up, so you nod to your co-leader to structure things a bit. The co-leader writes the name of the activity on the blackboard, then asks if anyone knows what that is. He explains what it is in simple terms, and shows a sample. He reminds the group about the two patients' interests in gardening and says this activity is similar. He asks who has ever planted a houseplant before. By this time, we are ready to demonstrate the steps. The co-leader writes them down briefly on the board as we talk and demonstrate.

All is going okay except Max just sits there unless someone reminds him to do each step. Meanwhile, Mike has finished pouring all his colored sand. He wants to do another one. We ask him if he could help Maria instead. She is slightly shaky and afraid she'll spill too much. He is happy to have a special job. The student then cues Max so he will continue.

The dirt is too messy for Maria. She doesn't want to touch it. She gives it to Mike to fix. Mike finishes his, hers, and spills some more, which he then is encouraged to clean up. The planting goes fairly smoothly. The co-leaders assist as needed. The student asks who knows how to take care of the plant. Steve, who likes to garden, gives a lengthy but accurate description. The leader rephrases it in a few sentences.

Evelyn volunteers how pretty these look. Building on her comment we ask each person to hold theirs up so we can compliment them. We start to talk about what it means to take care of something like a plant, the responsibility and the need for just enough water and light.

One leader feels inspired for the wrap-up and instead of the planned activity, asks who feels cared for in this group. Several patients raise their hands. Evelyn says it felt nice to make these. We then ask people to say what they liked about the group today. We write their answers on the board.

In the post-group meeting the leaders discussed how the group was more warm and expressive than usual. It almost went better than expected. We think it was because we planned well in terms of supplies and structure and also adapted on the spot by adjusting the pace, offering guidance to individuals to complete the task or help each other as needed, and raising simple discussion topics.

Changing the Activity and Its Presentation

Sometimes more adaptations are needed. You may need to change the order of activities which are planned or pick new ones altogether. You review your criteria for change — that is, the group needs you are perceiving. Consider if you need more or less structure, action, verbal interaction, movement, self-expression, or fun. Then change the nature of the activity accordingly. If you have been sitting, maybe you need an activity for which you can stand. If you have been interactive, maybe you need some time to solve problems. If things have become very tense, maybe you need to create some space and levity. To change an activity on the spot requires a thorough knowledge of other options and having supplies stored in the same room so you can switch gears quickly.

Once you have an activity in progress, sometimes only minor adjustments are needed to maintain the interest and evoke new behaviors of the group members. You can consider factors such as complexity, novelty, and uncertainty.

Complexity. Complexity involves the number of directions, the amount of skill required, the difficulty of comprehension of the concepts, and the length of time to attend to the task. If patients seem to be hesitating to respond or are giving some other indicator of being overwhelmed with the task, see if you need to vary the complexity. Consider breaking down the steps into smaller units, making the rules easier, moving the target closer, or making the game end sooner.

As an example, Terry was acutely psychotic on admission and could only stay in the group 15 minutes initially. Frequently she would pace around the room and stare into space. However, by holding her hand and guiding her, she would sit down and join the group when doing simple movement exercises. Asking her to lead a movement would be too overwhelming for her, but we noticed her rocking back and forth and asked the group to build on that movement. Similarly, when the group was making tissue paper flowers, she was given yarn to wrap around a can which was used as the vase. Making flowers was too complex, yet wrapping yarn capitalized on her ability to move repetitively and challenged her to focus on an object. In this way, she was still included in the group activities in a way that met her individualized needs and did not set her apart from others.

Novelty. Novelty involves the tension between familiarity with the activity and newness. Patients in Directive Group usually respond best to activities which build on familiar activities and are then varied. If every day you did the same balloon exercise, selected activities, and wrap-up activities, you could be sure the group would not last long. Also, if every day you had a different order of activities and nothing predictable, you would not have much of a stable group left. You can rely on the basic sequence of activities to provide familiarity, but then you need to vary the specifics to enhance novelty. If the group seems bored, you need to start being more creative.

Uncertainty. The element of chance, is often a component of games. When thought of as a separate entity, it too can be graded within an activity. If it is obvious what the word is for a game of hangman, or who is "it" in follow the leader, or who will win Chinese checkers, then there is too much certainty and irritation will set in. If no one knows how to play a game, or can guess what someone is acting out in charades, or doesn't understand why a certain patient's helpless demands are continuously being ignored by the leaders, then there is too much uncertainty and the anxiety of the group will rise.

Reviewing the Process for Adapting Activities

Clinical judgment develops from experience. By reflecting on what you learned after each group, you start to see patterns and organizing principles. These influence your rational processes in preparing for the next group by having appropriate supplies for activities available. You also realize the need to have analyzed each activity thoroughly so you know what each contributes to skill development.

Then, with this reservoir of knowledge and resources in your repertoire, you rely on your perceptive processes to identify the needs of the group. You also generate criteria for meeting those needs. You stimulate your creative juices by asking questions about what would fill the needs. Your inner attitude is exploratory and gentle.

Once you come up with solutions, your rational processes evaluate the extent to which they serve the purpose for which they were intended. The cycle repeats endlessly. This happens very quickly — more quickly than it takes to explain the process.

References

1. Ornstein, R. (1972). The Psychology of Consciousness. Middlesex, England: Penguin Books.
2. Tuckman, B., Jensen, M. (1977). Stages of small group development revisited. Group Org Studies 2(4):419-427.

Suggested Reading

Arieti, S. (1976). Creativity: The Magic Synthesis. New York: Basic Books.

Berlyne, D. (1960). Conflict, Arousal and Curiosity. New York: McGraw-Hill.

Bruner, J. (1973). The organization of early skilled action. Child Develop 44:111.

Buzan, T. (1974). Using Both Sides of Your Brain. London: E.P.Dutton.

Csikszentmihalyi, M. (1975). Beyond Boredom and Anxiety. San Franscisco: Jossey Bass.

Cubie, S. (1985). Occupational analysis. In Kielhofner, G. (Ed.): A Model of Human Occupation: Theory and Application. Baltimore: Williams & Wilkins, pp. 147-155.

Cynkin, S. (1979). Occupational Therapy: Toward Health Through Activities. Boston: Little, Brown & Co.

May, R. (1975). The Courage to Create. New York: Bantam Books.

CHAPTER 9

HOW DO I START?
Fitting Directive Group into Your Program

If you believe that Directive Group would meet a need in your program, you have to think through how to introduce the idea so that it can be supported and successfully implemented. Initiating a Directive Group, as with any innovation, is really an attempt to change your program. Programs are made up of people, and people often experience resistance to change. Fear of the unknown is often cited as the reason, but sometimes the reason is a misconception of what is known. Fear of pain may be the real culprit, causing fantasies to abound about how much loss and readjustment will be required.

Fitting Directive Group into an existing group treatment program may affect only a few people, causing a minimum number of ripples of resistance. The next chapter is about affecting the program as a whole. Since the implications for that extent of change are greater, I will discuss a context for the change process in Chapters 10 and 11.

This chapter is restricted to describing the alterations of Directive Group you can make to meet the realities of your setting. It also considers the changes you might make in your program to support the essence of Directive Group. The rationale for making modifications is the issue. Features which can be modified include the norms of your setting, the adequacy of the environment, the availability of your staff, and your particular patient characteristics. You may also want to think about evaluating the effectiveness of the group at the onset.

Norms of Your Setting

One of the most important factors for integrating the Directive Group approach into your setting is to determine whether group therapy is a valued treatment approach by your staff. If group work is seen as integral to the total treatment program, than adding one more group of perceived value should be relatively easy to do. Indicators of valuing group work include honest attempts at the following practices:

-Not taking patients out of groups (i.e., for individual therapy, tests, or medications) unless absolutely necessary

-Not scheduling overlapping groups (i.e., groups that could include the same patients and thus cause a conflict)

-Staff routinely expecting and encouraging patients to attend groups (i.e., helping the most disorganized patients get to them)

-Discussing with patients what has occurred in groups during individual therapy and with staff during team meetings (i.e., interest shows support)

-Trainees taking advantage of opportunities to learn group dynamics and assist in leading groups.

If practices like these are not common in your setting, then you have some decisions to make. You have three choices: forget Directive Group and forge ahead with your current program (i.e., accept status quo); leave your present job and find a more congenial setting (i.e., reject status quo); or pull up your boots, roll up your sleeves, and get ready for a long haul at attempting to influence the system (i.e., you guessed it — change the status quo). If you attempt this track, you have your work cut out for you. More about this in the next chapter.

No matter what your situation, you can have an active role in attempting to influence those around you. Norms get shaped over time through a process of negotiation. You can't demand changes, but you can ease into them by letting others know what you want and letting them respond. For example, if you would like your groups to be part of a schedule of balanced activities, then ask other group leaders if they would be willing to schedule groups during other time slots. When someone takes a patient from your group for an appointment, follow up afterwards. Let the individual know, for instance, that you understand that the medical examination was important, but the group is also part of the patient's treatment plan and important in its own way.

Demonstrating respect for your own work as well as the work of others goes a long way towards creating good will and a positive therapeutic environment. Maybe you'll feel that you are extending yourself more than you think you should have to, but no one else will do it for you. It's too easy to build resentment because you make assumptions about another professional's motives when things don't go as you expected. Of course, if you level with people, you might be surprised to hear things about yourself or your department as well. Then again, the opportunity for close work relationships is increased when you establish a basis for communicating. Changes in ward attitudes and policies can happen, but they take time and consistent effort. To be successful in a delicate situation, see yourself as representing multiple roles — not only group leader, but also educator, patient advocate, interdisciplinary staff member, change agent, and diplomat. These are not "extras," but an essential part of your responsibilities as a flexible, thinking, caring professional.

Setting Up a Referral System

If your unit has a system for referring patients to groups, then you can probably adapt the Directive Group referral criteria to that system. Likewise, your system for documentation and communication can be expanded to include information from Directive Group. If you don't have a referral system, this might be one of the first places to instigate a change. It is fairly obvious that not all patients need a group like Directive Group. So, figuring out how to quickly and accurately identify those patients who would be likely to benefit should be relatively easy to do.

Initially, I thought the occupational therapy department should evaluate every patient who was admitted and tell the team who needed which type of group treatment. However, when Directive Group was designed, our 34 to 1 patient to occupational therapy staff ratio would have restricted me to evaluation only. This didn't make sense to me. What evolved was a referral system which turned out to be more ideal than my initial expectation because of the way it involved staff.

The referral form criteria are designed by the group leaders in consultation with the occupational therapy department and director of the unit. A member of the patient's team fills it out. Having a psychiatrist or nurse available to fill out the form has several benefits. First, since they provide 24-hour care for the patients, they see the patients whenever they are admitted and can provide a faster referral than if the patients had to wait to be seen by the occupational therapy staff. Although the decision to refer a patient is a shared team decision, the staff who has thought through the patient's needs can expedite the team's decision-making process. Second, the staff get involved in the patient's total treatment plan by writing the referrals at the same time they also prescribe medication, schedule family visits, and decide about the ward structure. In this way, the group program is not isolated from other aspects of the therapeutic environment.

The disadvantages of this process are occasional role blurring and loss of decision-making control. In order to have role flexibility, there is duplication of functions by different people, by definition. Sometimes this leads to lack of clarity about who is accountable for specific responsibilities. But it also means that vacations are easier to cover and team functioning is less dependent on certain people than on the filling of certain roles. The loss of decision-making control is most acute for the occupational therapy staff who would like to insist that a patient be referred to Directive Group. In this process, occupational therapists have input, just like any other team member and, because of their intimate relationship with the group program, are most often listened to. In 6 North's experience, very little time is lost in inefficient decision-making or disagreement over referral to this group. However, the discussions that do occur are usually necessary for optimum patient care. They also serve as informal inservice education.

Adequacy of the Environment

On the practical side, do you have a room for Directive Group? You don't need a lot of space, but it is best to have a room that is used routinely for the group. The room should have a door to provide privacy and a sense of security to the patients. Having a legitimate time and place for the group enhances its value to the patient and staff community. A consistent time is best for the patients because the predictability helps them reorganize their thought processes. However, having variable times that are well advertised and supported by staff is reasonable. Certainly, providing the group at a minimally acceptable level is better than not having the group at all.

In terms of the room itself, it needs to be large enough for several movable tables with a dozen or so easy-to-store chairs. A sink and blackboard are useful, as are storage cabinets for craft supplies, balls, and games. Most of the activities are adaptable from the supplies of the activity program, so the budget for the group need not be extensive. Special supplies might include a poster-size list of goals prepared by the audiovisual department, graduation awards and certificates of participation, and an inflator for the large balloons.

Patients are usually too disorganized to do group activities off the unit, and food-related activities have been only minimally successful with this group. This came as a surprise to us because we thought they would feel nurtured and enjoy feeding themselves. However, patients seem to be too needy to be interested in preparing food, and at times, too preoccupied to eat treats that are freely offered.

Availability of Staff

Leading groups is cost-effective in that you can treat more patients at one time. On the other hand, you must factor in the hidden costs of preparation time, documentation, and communication for more than one leader. Nevertheless, for this type of group you can't afford not to have co-leaders.

One of the hardest things might be to find them. If interdisciplinary staff already co-lead groups, then finding interested people may take some inservice education, informal communication, and friendly lobbying — but it can be done. If norms for co-leadership are not presently in place, there are still other options.

You can ask for a volunteer from the nursing staff to help you, and if necessary, a different person each time you meet. Even though you are taking them away from typical nursing duties, you are also decreasing the amount of disruption on the unit by having all the disorganized patients in one place for 45 minutes.

Or use each session as an experiential inservice training for staff and students of all disciplines. You prepare them for what to expect and emphasize the need for them to be playful and active so as not to intimidate the patients. In this way you have healthy adults who can follow your lead during the session to rely on for interaction. You also provide the staff and students with a valuable training experience.

Or you can see if other students would like to have group therapy experience. You could provide group supervision to social work, psychology, or medical students who are interning on your unit in exchange for their regular participation in the group. Not many people know how to work with such dysfunctional patients in ways other than verbal therapy, which is not usually very effective. The benefit for the student is to ensure patient contact, increase therapy skills, and learn to assess and treat patients from a focus on their functional capacities rather than pathologies.

When we first started Directive Group, we met three times a week. One day it was in the morning, the next in the afternoon, and the third day was during the evening in order to accommodate the nursing shift schedules. A psychiatric technician consistently co-led for a six-month period and then rotated with someone else. Eventually, the staff wanted the group to meet for five days a week. I felt that that was too much for me to do and there wasn't enough nursing support for it. The medical director of the unit then said he would co-lead the group with me. Even though it seemed unusual for a psychiatrist to be throwing balloons and doing activities, he believed in the underlying functional approach. It was therapeutic for staff as well as patients to realize he was so human, caring, and playful. What a status booster to the program, too!

The point is, you never know how your group will evolve. Much depends on the particular constellation of your setting and the personalities and preferences of the people involved. But if you aim in the direction you want to go, do a competent job at it, and are open to suggestions from others, you may be surprised at the support you get and the way in which your ideas develop.

Modifications for Various Patient Populations

During the six years I was involved with this group, I wrote various unpublished papers trying to describe the group. These were circulated to fellow students and clinicians. In addition, I gave numerous workshops on the Directive Group. The upshot was that the group was initiated in various settings in supportive treatment programs and on a trial basis during internships.

I learned about some of the modifications made in the group for the different patient populations and settings. For instance, in a long-term facility, with nursing home residents or chronic psychiatric patients, the group needed an arbitrary starting and stopping date. Some of the settings had patients in the group for three months before disbanding that group and starting with another group of patients. These settings have a majority of the patients who are appropriate for the group, so priorities have to depend on which dozen or so patients attend at any given period.

Offering the group four times a year changes the group from an open group to a closed group. The obvious advantage is in the ease in which continuity and cohesion can be established. The disadvantage is in the stability of the patient mix. If there is not a range of personalities and energy levels within the group, it is harder to move the members along the path to functional behavior. Expectation for goal attainment moves at a somewhat slower pace. Therefore, in addition to the referral criteria, co-leaders need to screen patients for compatibility.

When the group was modified for mentally retarded adults, the co-leaders changed the group from 45 minutes to a half hour. The sequence of activities remained the same, but the selection tended to emphasize short games and de-emphasize word games and discussion. The playful context was maintained, but, as might be expected, subtle differences were made in terms of how the co-leaders and patients related. For instance, there was more need for repetition during activities and less time for verbal interaction during the wrap-up.

The group was used successfully with neurologically impaired adults who suffered head injuries and stroke. Fewer patients were in the group because of the space taken up by wheelchairs. Also, more adaptations were made in the activities because of increased physical and perceptual limitations. However, the emotional support that the group offered the members was substantial and an unusual part of the rehabilitation program.

We have had blind and hearing-impaired patients in the short-term unit group. These patients not only benefit from the stimulation of the group, but they have a positive effect on the group in a way not initially anticipated. At first, the co-leaders looked at the adaptations as extra work and were afraid the other patients would resent the extra attention these patients required. But the modifications required an emphasis on clear communication and ways to learn basic skills. Somehow the process added a dimension of humanity to all the members and co-leaders — a grand equalizer, if you will.

Other Modifications

If you decide to initiate a Directive Group in your setting, there are other aspects you may want to modify. You can adapt the activities used in the group to better meet the cultural backgrounds and values of your patients. Once you know who the patients are, you can change the goals of the group to make them more relevant. You already know how to write referral criteria that most quickly identify those patients needing the group. Now if you think about those behaviors which are most problematic for the patients when they are in the group, you can form your own baseline assessment.

These types of changes would likely have an impact on your methods for monitoring and documenting patient progress. One setting added a dimension on the rating scale for memory impairment. Another focused on the routine evaluation of frustration tolerance. You will want to phrase your clinical notes to conform to standards for third-party reimbursement and hospital accreditation and to integrate this treatment into your billing system. This could be, for example, in the room rate, in a separate bill as a group, or converted to units of contact (e.g., segment the type of skills developed in the group by 15-minute intervals) as described on your billing form.

Likewise, you can articulate the rationale for Directive Group from a different frame of reference. It should be one that is compatible with the treatment philosophy of your setting and the problems and goals of the patients. I recommend the model of human occupation for the reasons explained in Chapter 2. However, I realize that there are many factors involved in selecting a specific theoretical base or in operating from an eclectic one. From my own experience, thinking through the theory and applying it in practice is not a one day proposition. Give yourself time to work through the issues while gaining experience leading the group. The more the group makes sense to you, the easier it will be to lead it, market it, and research it.

Program Evaluation

There are several ways to evaluate the effectiveness of Directive Group. First, the rating scale for individual patient monitoring gives concrete evidence of progress. Comparison of initial and outcome ratings for all patients seen in a designated amount of time, say six months, demonstrates the extent of change in patient behavior during the course of the group. This information can be useful for documenting accountability, need for more staff, and overall program development.

Second, quality assurance studies could be used to develop consensus around clinical judgment issues, such as how much progress (i.e., how many average points on the rating scale) is sufficient to justify continuation or expansion of the program. You could set standards for measuring successful outcomes and for the acceptable percentage of patients referred from the target population. You could also document the impact of actions taken to improve the group.

Third, clinical research studies provide a mechanism for evaluating the effect of the group. For example, in facilities in which a group is already in existence for the level of patients treated in Directive Group, the existing group could be compared with the Directive Group in the form of an outcome study. Patients referred for this level group could be randomly assigned to either group. The rationale would be that neither group has been proven effective, so that offering patients either condition would be ethical and as likely to be in their best interest. In settings where the choice is Directive Group or no treatment, then withholding treatment is more problematic.

Fourth, some inferences can be made from existing research studies about effective aspects of the Directive Group. For instance, groups designed for the psychotic population have been found to be most effective when they rely on structured activity and reality-based approaches.[1,6] One study suggested that groups with an intense interpersonal focus may be harmful.[5] Groups are more effective when combined with other forms of treatment, such as psychopharmacology and individual treatment.[7] However, drugs and psychotherapy alone are insufficient for developing social and occupational skills.[6,4] These studies, combined with studies which support the efficacy of brief hospitalization,[2,3] are not inconsistent with the principles of Directive Group. Obviously, research specifically designed to measure this group's effectiveness is necessary before causal inferences can be made.

References

1. Bendar, R., Lawlis, G. (1971). Empirical research in group psychotherapy. In Bergen, A.E., Garfield, S.L. (Eds.): Handbook of Psychotherapy and Behavior Change. New York: John Wiley & Sons, pp. 812-838.
2. Decker, J. (1972). Crisis intervention and prevention of psychiatric disability: A follow-up study. Am J Psychiatry 129:25-29.

3. Hertz, M., Endicott, J., Spitzer, R. (1977). Brief hospitalization: A two year follow-up. Am J Psychiatry 134:502-507.

4. Keith, S. (1982). Drugs: Not the only treatment. Hosp Commun Psychiatry 33:793.

5. Linn, M., Caffey E., Klett, C., et al. (1976). Day treatment and psychotropic drugs in the aftercare of schizophrenic patients. Arch Gen Psychiatry 36:1055-1066.

6. May, P. (1976). When, what, and why? Psychopharmacology and other treatments in schizophrenia. Compr Psychiatry 17:683-693.

7. Parloff, M., Dies, R. (1977). Group psychotherapy outcome research. Int J Group Psychotherapy 27:281-319.

Suggested Reading

Documentation and Accountability

Joe, B & Ostrow P (1987). Quality Assurance Monitoring in Occupational Therapy. Rockville, MD: American Occupational Therapy Association.

Hargreaves, W, Attkisson C, & Sorensen, J (Eds.) (1977). Resource Materials for Community Mental Health Program. U.S. Department of Health, Education, and Welfare. Rockville, MD: American Occupational Therapy Association.

Kuntavanish, A (1987). Occupational Therapy Documentation: A System to Capture Outcome Data for Quality Assurance Program Promotion. Rockville, MD: American Occupational Therapy Association.

Uniform Terminology for Reporting Occupational Therapy Services. (1979). Rockville, MD: American Occupational Therapy Association.

Waskow, I. & Parloff, M. (eds) (1975). Psychotherapy Change Measures. Rockville, MD: NIMH

Marketing

Conner, R & Davidson, J (1985). Marketing Your Consulting and Professional Services. New York: John Wiley and Sons.

McCaffrey, M (1983). Personal Marketing Strategies. Englewood Cliffs, New Jersey: Prentice-Hall.

Olson, T & Urban, C (1985). Marketing. The Occupational Therapy Manager (pp. 123-125). Rockville, MD: American Occupational Therapy Association.

Winston, J (1986). Marketing planning for psychotherapy group practices. Journal of Marketing for Mental Health, 1(1), 35-45.

Research Resources

Mattes, J, Rosen, B & Klein, D (1977). Comparison of the clinical effectiveness of "short" vs. "long" stay psychiatric patients. Journal of Nervous and Mental Disease, 165, 395-402.

Metzoff, J & Kornreich, M (1970). Research in Psychotherapy. New York: Atherton.

Moriarity, J (1976). Combining activities and group psychotherapy in the treatment of chronic schizophrenia. Hospital and Community Psychiatry, 27, 574-576.

Mosher, L & Keith, S (1979). Research on the psychosocial treatment of schizophrenia: A summary report. American Journal of Psychiatry, 136, 623-631.

Ostrow, P & Kaplan K (1987). Occupational Therapy in Mental Health: A Guide to Outcomes Research. Rockville, MD: American Occupational Therapy Association.

Stotsky, B & Zolik E (1965). Group psychotherapy with psychotics, a review -1921-1963. International Journal of Group Psychotherapy, 17, 321-344.

CHAPTER 10

WHAT IF WE WANT MORE?
Conceptualizing a System of Group Treatment

This chapter is geared largely to students, new therapists, and tentative innovators. I have an empathy for you as you begin to develop your sense of autonomy and professionalism. During my experiences teaching and supervising, I heard firsthand about many of your struggles to conceptualize your work, feel comfortable with your new responsibilities, and gain a perspective on the process of change. I have included many personal examples in the sections below in an attempt to demystify program development and to help those of you who feel isolated not to feel so alone.

Levels of Program Planning

The success of Directive Group relies on the context in which it occurs. A treatment group is only a part of a whole set of therapies. The group takes place on a specific unit of a particular facility in a certain community. Although not immediately obvious, each of these settings has an influence on the way in which the treatment program develops.

Imagine each setting as a series of concentric circles (Figure 10-1). Individual treatment is in the center, followed by Directive Group, then the occupational therapy and activity-oriented groups, then the whole group treatment program, the facility, the community, and finally the state and national health care system. You can choose to focus on the Directive Group or any of the circles. Each level of concern incorporates different problem definitions and solutions. For instance, national health care focuses on the current budget deficit and proposals for policies which can decrease the cost of health care while providing adequate services.

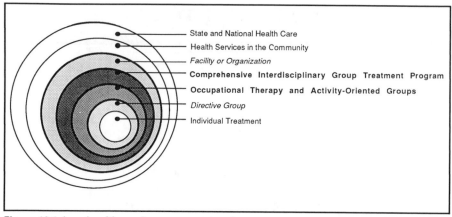

Figure 10-1. Levels of focus for program planning.

This chapter is directed toward thinking about a comprehensive group treatment program as well as planning an occupational therapy or activity-oriented group program. The next chapter is focused on planning and conceptualizing an interdisciplinary system of groups (including group psychotherapy). This gives a developmental approach to thinking about program development, from the Directive Group to the professional department in which it is resides.

Thinking for each level requires a different view of the world than the previous level. Your emphasis is no longer only on those areas which you know well and over which you have a reasonable sphere of control; the emphasis moves on to the larger system in which you learn about the coordination and cooperation necessary to work as a cohesive whole. Inclusion of issues from broader levels of conceptualization requires data about your facility, community, and state and national funding policies. In addition, the design of your group program will be affected by the individual patients who are admitted to the unit. How this works will be explained as we look at your program.

A Personal Perspective on Professional Growth

Thinking of your program as a system is a developmental stage for the relatively new therapist. When you are learning to become a mental health professional, there is so much information to master, it is often hard to synthesize it. For the occupational therapy practitioner, be it the professional or technical level, knowledge is sometimes compartmentalized into "peds" and "phys dys" and "neuro." The separation is a feature of most educational programs in order to package information for specific classes, time slots, and semesters. This makes some sense, but it gives the false impression that information and life in general are neat and tidy. It is as if the material does not interconnect with other aspects, as if it really has a start and finish.

So you go on internships to further integrate theory and practice. There you interact with real people who are patients and try to relate their medical and psychiatric symptoms to what you learned in school. You try to see what occupational therapy can do for their functional problems. If this was all you had to learn, it eventually would be manageable. But then you realize you have a supervisor to deal with, team members from other disciplines to learn about, procedures to follow, groups to lead, notes to write, projects to complete, and pretty soon it is overwhelming.

Focusing on your patients and your groups and your job makes the most sense. You pull in the reins so that you can master an area. As you did in school, you arbitrarily put boxes around certain areas and concentrate on learning what is in those boxes. That is why it is an indication of the next developmental stage to be able to notice the environment around you and not have to shut yourself off from it in order to cope. You somehow have integrated enough information, know-how, and confidence to see that what you do is an integral part of the whole occupational therapy department. As you relax more, you can see your department as part of the interdisciplinary program. These realizations are often like "ah ha's" and you remember the moment you felt differently about who you were and what you were doing professionally. You will know when you feel internally ready to have a different perspective because you will suddenly see you are part of a system.

I remember being in a managers meeting, where leaders of all the professions on the unit were represented, working on how to improve the program. I was rather worn out from trying to lead as many groups as possible because I was the only occupational therapist. I also was on every task group because whenever the director said we needed an interdisciplinary group, I felt obligated to represent the profession.

All of a sudden, it occurred to me that I didn't have to do more personally. I could use my knowledge of occupational therapy and apply it to the program as a whole. I could suggest how to implement principles, such as having a balance of work and play activities on the unit, throughout all of the treatment groups. My vantage point changed from straight ahead to being above my little problems and seeing a broader sphere of influence. It was akin to being involved with sibling rivalry problems, but then seeing the possibility for family cooperation and a sense of community. It's like when a musician realizes on a deeper level what it means to be part of the symphony. This is what a systems perspective means: not only, but also.

Context for Change

Systems thinking helps us realize that a change in one part of an organism effects the whole. What I like about systems theory is that the same ideas that we used to understand individual and group functioning can now be used to think about the whole organism (i.e., your facility). That is why being a catalyst for change in your program is ultimately an attempt to alter the culture of the whole ward.

In business circles much is written about strategic planning and corporate cultures which has relevance here. Rosabeth Moss Kanter talks of the "Change Masters" who are successful architects of organizational change.[1] They start with discovering the history of past changes in the organization;

not only the events that happened, but also the myths and symbols that were constructed. This awareness lays the foundation for creating new models of change based on lessons learned. In addition, she cites five building blocks for increasing an organization's capacity to change:

1. Departure from tradition. Looking for examples of unplanned small change efforts which were successful and using them to highlight the potential for continued experimentation. Then catalog the strengths in the organization, not the problem areas.

2. Crisis or galvanizing event. Taking advantage of unanticipated demands from the environment or management (such as a lawsuit or a new technology) which require a quick response. The more the organization has an integrated, not isolated, approach to crises, the more nontraditional strategies can be implemented.

3. Strategic decisions. Leaders in the organization articulating a vision out of which strategies are formulated. The possibilities inherent in new ideas are easier to recognize when this conceptual stage is in place.

4. Individual prime movers. Someone who is identified with pushing a new practice by communicating about it every chance he or she gets. People in the role of "idea champion" arouse commitment to change.

5. Action vehicles. Working out the concrete structures and patterns for the change. Mechanisms that fit the realities of the organization soon become "institutionalized" and represent the values of the setting.

These building blocks are quite relevant to the challenge of creating a comprehensive group treatment program. First of all, you can see that a prime mover is necessary, and that may be YOU. Do you have the time, skills, interest, and energy required for this job? If not, who can take on this role? Whoever the person is, he or she had better develop a network of supporters who have gleaned a thorough knowledge of the history of change in the facility. Then they can be ready to take advantage of environmental forces which come up (e.g., a new policy advocating clinical research or demands for improving the fiscal standing of the department) and insert the new group program as a remedy.

Second, do you have a strong leader who is making strategic decisions? Is there a vision for the treatment program in which your ideas about groups are a natural part? If not, what kind of grassroots work can be done to develop such a mind-set?

Third, have you done your homework on the mechanics of setting up a system of groups? Some of this needs to be done with others and will be addressed in Chapter 11. The remainder of this chapter focuses on the aspects you can think through alone when planning an occupational therapy or activity-oriented group program.

Identifying Patient Needs

Group treatment is a solution to a problem. If groups are the answer, what is the question? Patient needs. How can we best identify and meet patient needs? Too often, therapists come armed with their bag of tricks and try to inflict them on unsuspecting souls. That may be a little strong, but the issue is not only to give what you have, but to give what is needed. It is a process of negotiation. You can't offer a treatment you are not qualified to give, but neither should you offer something which isn't necessary just because you know how to do it and enjoy doing it. This predicament is similar to teachers who teach in the style they best learn, rather than use a range of approaches which are more facilitative of the students' learning styles.

You can assess patient needs in many ways. Usually it is best to get information from many sources, such as the patients themselves, other staff members, and documentation about the facility and community at large. You want to get a sense of how the patients and other people perceive the needs of the patients and compare this with as objective information as possible from historical data and your own evaluation.

You know you are ready to plan your program when you see patterns in the data you have collected. You can think through your patient population's needs by categories and choose the groups that will meet the most frequent and pressing needs.

Identifying Your Theoretical Framework

How you identify patient needs depends on your assessment tools. Your assessment tools are based on your theoretical frame of reference, the questions you want answered, and your professional training. Depending on your professional discipline, special areas will require evaluation, such as family dynamics, the leisure lifestyle, or movement experiences. Likewise, some professions advocate assessing a wide range of areas, even if there are no services available. On the other hand, the demands of the setting may impose time and philosophical constraints.

As an occupational therapy practitioner, you probably want to know how well the person is functioning now, how well they used to do, and what direction they would like to go in the future. If you are using the model of human occupation, you want to know the functioning of each patient's subsystem as well as his or her expected environment upon discharge. You will need to find out about values and goals, habits, roles, and skills. If you are using a functional performance framework, you may emphasize daily living and vocational skills more extensively. If you are operating from a sensory integrative or a cognitive disability frame of reference, you will use very different tools.

Clearly, the assessment procedure is an ongoing process. When you start your job, you may draw on your familiarity with certain instruments and evaluate patients with an interest checklist, observation on a task, and an interview. After a month of evaluations, you reflect on how these real patients responded to your procedure. You may notice most patients do not like the task and find the interview too long. So you modify the interview and offer a choice of three new tasks. Then you realize that one-third of your unit's population is elderly, and you decide you need to have special components of the assessment for them.

The reason it is important to realize why you are using the instruments you are using is because it will influence how you conceptualize the patients' needs. If you are looking for social skill deficits, you will find them. If you are not looking at sensory integrative functioning, then you are unlikely to think about a patient's problem with task performance in this way. What is important is to be explicit about what you are looking for and why. Since program development is an ongoing activity, you can change your procedures later if you are clear about what you have done and what remains to be explored. Further, your degree of sureness about what you are doing depends whether you are starting a new program, revising an established program, or changing the system in which the program exists.

Starting a New Program

When you start a new program, you have no previously established good will to build on. By the same token, you have no bad reputation to turn around or habits to undo. It is you, your ideas, and how you apply them to the patients and staff in the particular situation. When I was developing the program, I remember thinking it was important to establish the view that occupational therapy is a process, not an activity. It's not just that patients cook a meal, for instance. It's what happens during the planning, eating, and experiencing phases of the group effort; we learn about ourselves through the process.

Other than this overriding vision, the specifics of the program are to be determined. I started to figure out the specifics by learning who did what and where they perceived the gaps in the program. In this way I inadvertently learned about the history of the unit. I did not have much background then in change theory, so I used to follow my intuition and learned by trial and error. I am sharing some of my experiences to emphasize to those of you who might be doubting yourself about being an innovator that you can grow into this role.

When I first was hired on the inpatient unit, there was an art therapist, recreation therapy graduate student, a part-time dance therapist, and a nurse who did psychodrama. There was no coordinated activity oriented department. The psychiatrist who was the director of the unit wanted an occupational therapist on the unit to motivate patients. When he was on his residency, he was impressed with how the occupational therapist could get patients going. He wrote a grant for our unit and hired me.

Although I felt very wanted, I felt the need to prove myself so that the grant would be converted to a permanent position — which ended up taking several years and much toleration of frustration. In order to be accepted and decrease their resistance to change, I tried not to step on too many toes. I found a functional orientation was underemphasized in the program and yet consistent with my skills and philosophical bent. I began evaluating patients with tools I was familiar with which would give me information about their performance and goals. I also talked to patients about their perception of the program. I used an empirical approach. I changed theories like new clothes: I tried different ones on over the years to see how they fit. Some of them became whole wardrobes; others only lasted a season. I encourage those of you starting a new program to keep an open, exploratory attitude which allows you to discover over time different ways of thinking and working.

Revising an Established Program

When you are revising your own program, it is probably akin to taking nips and tucks in a dress that no longer fits, but is one you still like. You add shoulder pads and change the belt and it looks pretty good. Similarly, you add a group here, change the frequency of how often a group meets there, but the integrity of the program remains unchanged.

If you inherited someone else's program, you may have more dissonance with it. There may be parts that you see the benefit from, but you'd like to emphasize different skills or add a more standard evaluation component. You may want to change the whole theoretical orientation or increase the continuity of care. Even though you'd really like to get rid of the old dress and get a brand new one, you are used to the dress and reluctant to be drastically different. So you do major alterations step by step, changing the length, color, and bodice. You have, in effect, bought that new dress a little at a time. In other words, by mapping out the changes in the current program little by little, you can create a revised program more congruent with your values and goals. All it takes is patience, planning, persistence, and perspective.

Changing the System

What gets complicated is when you perceive that your program can't be as effective as you think it could be without changing the system in which it exists. For instance, you have the feeling everyone on the unit does his or her own thing, and are not that interested in how it all fits together. Staff complain informally about being isolated. Patients complain about the program being fragmented. You see lots of competition and turf fights over space, time, and budget. Staff are there to be helpful to patients, but somehow they are not helping each other.

This happened on the unit in which I worked. At first gripe sessions led to an allied health group in which we formally identified problems on the unit. This led to a realization we did not have a unifying philosophy of treatment. We discussed this during staff meetings and eventually the director of the unit authorized a group of interested staff to form a task group and work on developing a philosophical statement on behalf of the whole staff. Because we were a voluntary group, we had a large investment in the change process. The core of the group, two nurses, a social worker, and I became trusted friends. We proposed a biopsychosocial philosophy to the unit and wrote up a complete description of the program. The art therapist, therapeutic recreation specialist, psychologist, and each specialty area wrote their own parts, but all was edited by the core group for coherency.

Out of this process came the idea of a centralized referral system for each part of the program in order to emphasize an individualized approach to patient care. Also, we discussed the patients who were benefiting and those who did not seem to be getting as much as possible from the program. This is where the idea of Directive Group and the level system of groups was born.

The process whereby the referral system, levels of functioning, and addition of Directive Groups were established led to the formation of an integrated system of group treatment. Based on the perception of the prevailing ward culture, the occupational therapy and other activity-oriented groups were not isolated nor viewed as merely "nice, but not necessary." They became as integral to the group program as the verbal (supportive) group therapy and the community meetings. The low functioning groups were just as important as the high level groups. The group treatment program was valued as a whole just as individual psychotherapy and psychopharmacology were valued. It was gratifying to note the new program was recognized by the Department of Psychiatry, the local community, and various publications as being beneficial.

While all the changes could not have been predicted, the major program change was planned for and implemented. Does the picture sound too rosy? We had our share of blood baths and conflict, believe me. We struggled with team resistance, lack of respect from some of the medical hierarchy, loss of key employees, budget restrictions, and personality clashes. But remember what we learned from the "Change Masters" — building on strengths was more successful than a laundry list of troubles. Somehow we got where we were heading, not perfectly, not permanently, but sufficiently to put some desired changes in place and see their actual effect over time.

References

1. Kanter, R. (October 1983). Change masters and the intricate architecture of corporate culture change. Management Rev 18-28. Vol. 72.

Suggested Reading

Bair, J., Gray, M. (1985). The Occupational Therapy Manager. Rockville, MD: The American Occupational Therapy Association.

Cubie, S., Kaplan, K., Kielhofner, G. (1985). Program development. In Kielhofner, G. (Ed.): A Model of Human Occupation. Baltimore: Williams & Wilkins, pp.156-167.

Fidler, G. (1984). Design of Rehabilitation Services in Psychiatric Hospital Settings. Laurel, MD: RAMSCO.

Grossman, J., Bortone, J. (1986). Program development. In: Mental Health SCOPE: Strategies, Concepts, and Opportunities for Program Development and Evaluation, pp. 91-100. Rockville, MD: American Occupational Therapy Association.

Meyers, B. (1965). A Guide to Medical Care Administration 1:11-23. Washington, DC: American Public Health Association.

CHAPTER 11

HOW DO YOU DO IT?

Getting Practical About Comprehensive Program Development

Building on some of the ideas in Chapter 10, we can see that effective program change relies on people working together. Several distinct roles are necessary[3] as well as realistic plans based on the ward's strengths:

-An innovator who designs the new approach

-An advocate who lobbies for change

-The sponsor who facilitates the change process through politics and logistics

-The change agent who implements the change

-The consumers who benefit from the change

This book is based on personal experiences with comprehensive program planning in which Directive Group was the innovation in conjunction with the ideas for an integrated system of group treatment. Looking back on our change process, various staff stand out as having had key roles (some having more than one). As you have probably already guessed, I was the innovator. The group leaders who helped implement the change (myself included) were the change agents. The psychiatrist who is the director of the unit sponsored the change and was critical to the success of the program. The advocates were the task force members who articulated a philosophy for the unit and wrote the forms and documents reflecting the program changes. The patients benefited from the changes in which more individualized needs were met.

What About Politics?

It is beyond the scope of this book and my expertise to present an indepth discussion of issues of power, domination, repression, and control. However, what I do know is that they exist. Whenever there is unequal resource distribution, there will be conflict, turf battles, and attempts at manipulation.

People who view organizations from a political perspective don't see these trends as problems; rather they see them as natural and serving to balance power.[1] In addition to the hierarchical chain of command common in most organizations, the political framework emphasizes the influential roles of the informal leaders and decision-makers. Organizations are built upon coalitions of individuals who negotiate for mutual self-interests in the service of the overall organizational mission.

Inherent in being a "helping professional" is a strong bias for cooperation. We relentlessly strive for collaboration and conflict resolution. While these are worthy strivings, they have their limitations. Knowledge of other perspectives on organizations may help deal with the anxiety from unresolved conflict.

One maxim should be kept in mind as you decide where to put your energies regarding program change: scarcity of resources causes more jockeying for power.[2] Similarly, in your dealings with other staff, note that the more people perceive their self-interests as threatened, the greater their propensity to play political games. It follows that the more you can control critical resources, the more power you will have.

I believe there is a place for healthy competition. Shrinking financial resources are forcing health care providers to be more accountable for their programs. As more quality programs develop, more competent health care providers emerge. If you want to make a difference in this competitive environment, you have to be willing to think out your strategy, solicit support, and tackle resistance. The more knowledge mental health professionals have about the political, economic, and social forces which influence treatment programs, the more effective we can be in devising systems which support human function in concert with environmental realities. The remainder of the chapter addresses specific change processes and steps for implementation. The chapter concludes with general principles of programming which can easily be applied to a variety of short-term settings.

General Change Processes

Stay Constructive

Be willing to do something about problems; don't just complain. Talk about what is good in the program. Explain how you came to the conclusion that things could be improved. Share your thinking about unmet needs with others. Be sure to emphasize your vision of what you would like to see in the future.

Involve Others

Don't try to save the program yourself. If you work alone, you're likely to get scapegoated by the staff. You won't get all the glory and you will probably be an easy target for blame. Complex problems require the input from lots of people. Be a catalyst for getting people excited about what could be.

Have a Long-term Perspective

Focus on what you CAN do at each juncture; don't throw out the baby with the bath water. There is no perfect program, so don't feel as though you have to start from scratch. Make changes in the direction you are aiming for. You might not get all of what you want, but without consensus and cooperation, your gains are likely to be sabotaged. Be gentle. Everyone is as attached to their ideas as you are to yours, and who's to say who's right?

Have a Time Frame

Have a time frame, but within it, go with the flow. Give yourself enough time to be creative, and then to refine the ideas into concrete steps. Don't leave too much time or the natural resistance to change may override the press to finish. Remember, once the ideas are out, it takes more time than you might think to write them up. Arrange as soon as possible to get help from support staff and to get information on needed bureaucratic procedures, such as those related to devising new forms for the medical record.

For example, we started formally meeting in January and had the forms in place, group leaders selected, and the program ready to go by July 1 when the new psychiatric residents started their year rotation. The brainstorming and actual creation of the new program took about three months. We did a few all-nighters at the end of the six months to finish writing, typing, and editing.

Specific Change Processes

1. Gather Key Knowledgeable People

Key people, who are informed about, interested in, and affected by the proposed change, are your resources, support system, and potential allies. Competence breeds competence, so if at all possible make sure you have people together who really know about groups, patient needs, and program development. Energy and investment also go a long way to making the process meaningful and fun. People who might otherwise block your efforts due to fears, loss of power, or whatever, can be instrumental in converting major obstacles into opportunities. Bring your rivals into the process. Create bridges of understanding.

2. Brainstorm Freely; Make Lists

If you work better initially alone, review your documents and search your memory. Then gather as a group and compare notes. Discuss your observations. Let each of your opinions trigger new ideas. Write down what you discover. Don't try to be organized at first; the lists and ideas should flow. Later, patterns will emerge. Then you can sort into categories and set priorities. Essentially, play first; plan later.

3. Analyze the Information

In the information you have all gathered, look for patterns. Where are the gaps? What are the discrepancies between what is intended and what is actual?

A theoretical framework suggests categories for sorting needs; so does the scope of the profession, such as guidelines from an association on roles and functions of mental health practice. Clinical judgment and the information itself also are sources for conceptualizing clusters of needs.

4. Develop Criteria for Judging the Program

In our case, we wanted a program that was **individualized** to patient's needs. We also wanted a system which was **coordinated** and **cohesive**. We wanted an assortment of groups that met the **predominate needs** of the patient population. We wanted the groups to reflect **balance and variety**. We wanted the groups to be responsive to the different **levels of functioning** of the patients. We wanted to build in **flexibility** for minor changes in the population.

5. Compare the Program to Agreed-Upon Criteria

Sometimes it is useful to graphically represent the program to give you another chance to stand back and view the program critically. We used a diagram and a grid (Tables 11-1 and 11-3) to help evaluate the groups against the criteria for balance, variety, and patient levels.

6. Create New Alternatives; Plan the Program Change

Probably new ideas keep cropping up throughout the process of meeting, but formalize them by this point. What are the new groups needed? Which ones are repetitive and can be combined with others or disbanded? Which ones need a different focus or name? Which ones need different co-leaders? At this point you are looking for conceptual consistency. However, there are people behind each group or idea. Be diplomatic, politic, and kind.

You will actually be reworking this step and step 5 repeatedly until the pieces fall into place. Be sure to agree on the changes that must be made. You might get everything you are shooting for, but more likely your maximum objectives need a longer-term time frame. If it appears you won't be able to obtain at least the minimum changes you have identified, then it is not worth the time and energy to establish an unacceptable or inadequate program.

Let's go through some of the specific steps necessary to set up your program.

Steps for Comprehensive Program Planning

1. Identify Program Needs

Start with what you have going for you in the program. List all of the groups currently in progress. Who are they for? Who is responsible for leading them? What are the groups' purposes? How successful are they?

Think about the holes in the program. Look over your evaluations for the past six months. Are there any recurring problems which you identify but don't treat? Are there groups of patients by age or diagnosis which are routinely left out? Are the same patients in every group?

Talk to patients about the program. What are their opinions about the most useful groups? Are there any additions they would like to see? What do they think are the major problems?

Ask the staff who deal with patients' families if they have any observations to share. What about the attending physicians' experiences with the unit? They usually admit patients to several local hospitals so they may have some ideas from other programs.

2. Identify Staff Needs

Just because you think you have a handle on what the patients' needs are and how to meet them through the group program, doesn't mean this is the end of the story. What about the needs of the people who are going to be providing the service? Their needs are equally legitimate. Sure, you didn't go to school to learn to deal with staff, you went to help patients. But people are people, and what you give is often what you get. And what you give to patients is not often what you need.

I am reminded of watching the nurses who were assigned to the quiet room to observe highly disturbed patients. The nurses experienced the same isolation as the disorganized patients, but that was not necessary for the nurses' mental health; it was part of the job. But to the extent the tasks on the job do not meet a staff member's needs, is the extent to which other factors, such as peer support and after work let-down-your-hair sessions at the local bar, become important.

So talk and plan with other staff — the staff in your department and members of the other disciplines. Find out their time schedules, constraints, territorial issues, special strengths. When we first started Directive Group, in order to get the cooperation of nursing staff to help co-lead the group, we had the group three days a week, each time at a different time period. Even though disorganized patients can remember a group better at the same time each day, we felt it was more important to have the group co-led than to have it at a consistent time. By having one group in the morning, one in the afternoon, and one in the evening, shift schedules were more easily accommodated. In addition, nursing staff helped remind patients it was time for group, since they needed help and the staff knew we had considered their needs.

On 6 North, activity-oriented staff always led groups and the psychiatric residents led verbal group therapy. The change we made was to open up the group leadership role to all interested staff members. This made for flexibility when scheduling groups and more opportunities for staff to learn from each other. Primary leaders of groups were the ones best trained for the roles. In addition, the occupational therapist had a major role in writing the descriptions and referral forms for all of the groups and coordinating the group treatment program. In this way the occupational therapy program was thoroughly integrated into the group treatment program and, in fact, was largely responsible for the conceptualization and coordination of the program as a system.

3. Identify Administrative Support

What are your resources? Do you have the time, space, and budget to support the new changes? Maybe administration won't help you, but you don't want them to thwart you. What rules of the administration game do you have to play? Find out and do what you have to do — turn in forms in triplicate or use their computer system, whatever. Keep your eye on your goals and don't let minor annoyances distract you.

4. Identify the Broad Range of Needs

Based on the variety of patients we saw, we felt the group program should address needs across three broad areas: occupational functioning, interpersonal interaction, and mind/body integration. If you want to try this, draw three horizontal lines (Table 11-1).

Start with the occupational dimension. Work and leisure form the ends of a continuum in which both components are emphasized, but to different degrees in each group. Write down the groups that are more work-oriented at one end of a horizontal line. Write down the groups that are more leisure-oriented at the other. Some will fall in the middle and be a mix of both. Some groups are irrelevant to this dimension.

Now do the same thing for the interpersonal dimension. Which groups are more oriented towards social interaction and which are more common to intimate relationships?

The final dimension is the mind/body continuum. List the groups which are characterized by physical capacities at one end. List those that depend on cognitive abilities at the other. Now look at the configuration. Does it have

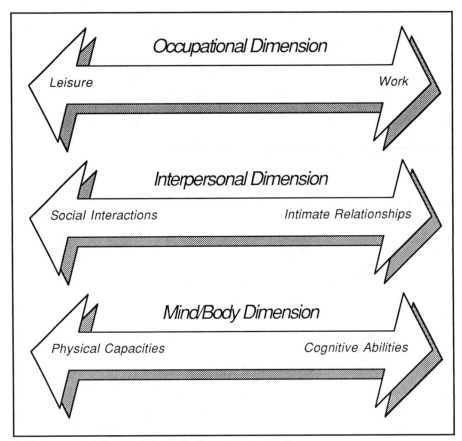

Table 11-1. Broad Range of Needs for Group Programming.

From Kaplan K. (1986) The Directive Group: Short-Term Treatment for Psychiatric Patients With a Minimal Level of Functioning. *AJOT, 40,*(70).

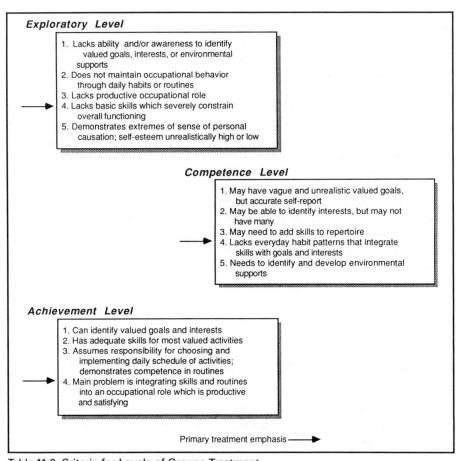

Exploratory Level

1. Lacks ability and/or awareness to identify valued goals, interests, or environmental supports
2. Does not maintain occupational behavior through daily habits or routines
3. Lacks productive occupational role
4. Lacks basic skills which severely constrain overall functioning
5. Demonstrates extremes of sense of personal causation; self-esteem unrealistically high or low

Competence Level

1. May have vague and unrealistic valued goals, but accurate self-report
2. May be able to identify interests, but may not have many
3. May need to add skills to repertoire
4. Lacks everyday habit patterns that integrate skills with goals and interests
5. Needs to identify and develop environmental supports

Achievement Level

1. Can identify valued goals and interests
2. Has adequate skills for most valued activities
3. Assumes responsibility for choosing and implementing daily schedule of activities; demonstrates competence in routines
4. Main problem is integrating skills and routines into an occupational role which is productive and satisfying

Primary treatment emphasis ⟶

Table 11-2. Criteria for Levels of Groups Treatment.
From Cubie, S. & Kaplan K. (1982) A Case Analysis Method for Model of Human Occupation. *AJOT, 36*(10).

balance? Is there coherence? Are their obvious gaps? Is the breadth of groups appropriate to the range of patient needs?

5. Identify Levels of Functioning

Before taking off on program planning, one other analysis should be considered. This is viewing the range of levels of functioning of the patient population. Usually, even if all the patients are the same diagnosis, there is a range of functioning because some patients are newly admitted and more dysfunctional, while other patients are more functional and are preparing for discharge. Most short-term units have patients with a wide range of diagnoses and problems, so that several levels of functioning are represented.

If you have criteria already established for the various levels, list them. If not, take a stab at jotting down the patient variations you have in your head and take for granted. Or take levels which other programs have established and see if they fit for your population. For instance, because some short-term units are admitting more chronically ill, revolving door patients, there tends to be a large middle group of functioning patients, with fewer high level functioning patients than previously. The criteria for levels is then a subdivision of the second group rather than the full range of functioning as articulated by the levels described in Table 11-2.

Once you have consensus on the levels, make a chart which lists the groups by the appropriate levels (Table 11-3). Because different disciplines were responsible for different groups, we also listed groups by profession. Whereas the exercise on dimensions established the **range** of groups, this exercise emphasizes the **depth** of the program. Similarly, whereas before you looked from a **horizontal** perspective, this is a **vertical** one.

Again, you are analyzing the number of groups at each level and the appropriateness of this constellation for your patient population. You may also be looking at the appropriateness and balance of the staff group leadership. Do you have sufficient numbers of groups for each level of functioning? Do you offer a gradation of experiences so that patients can progress throughout the program? Do you offer continuity of care from inpatient to day care and outpatient groups? Do you follow up? Once you have your program articulated and coordinated on paper, you still have to implement it. The following are some principles of programming that helped make our groups function comprehensively as a system.

Principles of Comprehensive Group Programming

1. Have a Structured Schedule

Post a schedule that blocks off the group times. By having set times for groups, stability is provided to the unit which helps to offset the otherwise fast and uneven pace of the short-term program. The process of agreeing on

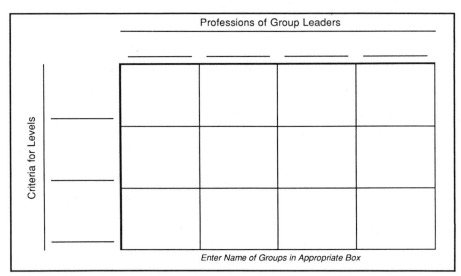

Table 11-3. Categorizing Groups by Levels of Functioning and Professional Discipline. From Kaplan K. (1986) The Directive Group: Short-Term Treatment for Psychiatric Patients With a Minimal Level of Functioning. *AJOT, 40*,(70).

which groups to offer at which times helps make group treatment a priority. The schedule makes it easier for staff to remind patients when it is time for a group and to plan other appointments, such as laboratory tests or giving medications, around group times. Be sure to avoid having groups which are appropriate for the same patients meet at the same times.

2. Maintain Clear Time Boundaries

Start and stop each group at the scheduled times. This helps the patients value the group as a special form of treatment. It is also helps disorganized patients get oriented to time and helps patients who are lax to develop habits of punctuality.

3. Set Reasonable Short-term Goals

The problems dealt with in each group should be achievable in a short time frame. They should be specific, behavioral, and understandable and important to the patients. Reasonable goals help maintain the morale of patients, their families, and the staff because they support the perception that changes are really happening. A major source of staff burn-out is a product of unrealistic goals. Being able to identify the "bottom-line" priorities and letting go of the rest is critical.

4. Review the Purpose of the Group Each Session

With so many patients being new to the groups, you can't repeat the purpose of the group too often. Even patients who have been there a while benefit from the repetition. Often, as they make progress on their goals and become more functional, they can relate their problems to the purpose of the group in a more meaningful way.

5. Make Each Session Complete Within Itself

Because of the short length of stay, you can't rely on the patients completing a sequence of sessions. This makes it essential to make each session count. Even if you have in mind a series of activities which would be optimal for each patient referred to the group, you have to plan each session so that a patient can benefit if only there for that one time.

6. Use Appropriate Activities

Again, because of the short time frame, you need to make your program as appealing and relevant to the patients as possible. You don't have time to correct too many mistakes or win patients back who have been turned off. Be sure to match the activities to the common patient problems and their backgrounds. Also, look for activities which are quick, safe, and portable.

7. View Each Group as a Creation of a Therapeutic Environment

Each group provides a way for patients to learn about themselves and make changes. The leaders help create these specially designed environments by deciding for each group how to titrate the optimal levels of arousal, help patients enhance their feelings of confidence and control, stimulate meaning and interest in the activities, and convey expectations relevant for patients' needs, goals, and roles.

8. Develop Active and Supportive Co-leaders

Co-leadership offers better continuity throughout the program and enhances interdisciplinary collaboration. It provides an excellent way to train staff and students in group techniques as well as familiarize them with the occupational therapy process. Co-leaders can share the responsibility for discussing patients in team meetings and documenting treatment progress.

9. Keep Evaluation an Ongoing Process

Review individual records of patient progress to make sure the patients are improving. Periodically, review each group to see if it is meeting its stated objectives. Then review the whole program to make sure the groups are still responsive to the needs of the patient population.

10. Maintain Flexibility

With a constant turnover of patients, change is the rule, not the exception. Be aware of outside factors influencing the groups, such as upcoming holidays and weekends, staff comings and goings, crises, and new students on rotation. Be ready to adapt as necessary by changing the time of a group, the activity which is planned, the themes discussed, or whatever else is appropriate. Keep in mind there are as many ways to do things as there are people. So don't worry if you can't do all of the things that are suggested here. I'd be concerned if you even wanted to. The important thing is to employ a "filter." Your filter allows you to screen what you need based on your time, energy, skills, and inclinations. The point is, it always gets back to YOU — your perceptions, beliefs, and feelings. That is why the concluding chapter in this book is devoted to the anxieties that plague us all, especially when we are new group leaders and therapists.

References

1. Bowman, L., Deal, T. (1984). Modern Approaches to Understanding and Managing Organizations. San Francisco: Jossey Bass.
2. Morgan, G. (1986). Images of Organization. Beverly Hills, CA: Sage.
3. OD Resources Inc. (1985). Atlanta.

Suggested Reading

Cohen, H. (1980). You Can Negotiate Anything. New York: Bantam Books.
Filley, A. (1975). Interpersonal Conflict Resolution. Glenview, IL: Scott, Foresman & Co.
Harragan, B. (1977). Games Mother Never Taught You: Corporate Gamesmanship for Woman. New York: Warner Books.

Harvey, J. (Summer 1974). The Abilene paradox: The management of agreement. Org Dynamics, pp.63-80, Vol. 3, $_1$.

Hennig, M., Jardin, A. (1977). The Managerial Woman. New York: Pocket Books.

Hertzman, M. (1984). A psychiatrist's experience with occupational therapy on a short-term general hospital unit. Occup Ther Ment Health 4(3):101-114.

LaBella, A., Leach, D. (1983). Personal Power: The Guide for Today's Working Woman. Boulder, Colorado: Newview Press.

Stone, J., Bachner, J. (1977). Speaking Up. New York: McGraw-Hill.

CHAPTER 12

YOU CAN DO IT!

Where You've Been and Where to Go from Here

Before delving into this final chapter, let's review where we have been. This book began with a metaphor of cooking to explain the process of learning to lead groups. The idea was offered that the more you know about cooking the more fun it is. So off you went to learn more about group leadership so that it too could be fun and rewarding.

First, you got advice to study group dynamics and gain some practical experience both participating in groups as a member and apprenticing as a leader. You were encouraged to understand normal and pathological behavior as it applies to your setting and yourself. You were given a context for thinking about how you learn best and for learning about Directive Group in a developmental sequence.

Next, we focused on describing the patients for whom Directive Group was designed. Addressing their minimal level of functioning, the essential components of the group format were presented. You were given some background on how the group was initially developed and later reconceptualized, using the model of human occupation as the theoretical framework.

A sense of how the Directive Group fit into the whole treatment process was presented next. You thought through different ways of identifying patient needs and followed a case example from admission to discharge.

After this, you were ready to learn how to organize Directive Group. You started by planning for the group within a sequence of events. Next you focused on structuring the group activities around the four group goals. Following another case example, you saw how the treatment process was implemented in Directive Group from the baseline assessment to the monitoring of progress and termination from the group. You then learned how to individualize patient goals and how to discharge a patient from the group when not making progress.

Finally, you were ready to focus on group leadership. You saw how to elicit interaction by being a role model and creating a playful context with your co-leader. Through offering choices and organizing space, you emphasized the values in the group for respect, support, and action.

You were aided in knowing what to expect from the group over the long haul through the description of four typical group sessions. Based on the phases of group development, you got a feel for how group needs get expressed. You were helped to deal with these needs through the concepts of adapting activities and finding optimal arousal levels. A planning worksheet and numerous examples were offered to stimulate your creativity. You were directed to the Appendix for a resource of additional activity ideas.

Now that you knew all about Directive Group, you were helped to think about the approach as an innovation. You saw yourself as a change agent with staff resistance and organizational issues to address. You examined the norms and structure of your facility to predict the ease of fitting the group into an existing program. Viewing your setting as a system, you used change concepts from the corporate sector to think through strategies for innovation. Additional guidelines helped you consider ways of collaborating with others to devise a complex plan and effectively implement your ideas for comprehensive group treatment.

So here we are. This book promised to help launch you on your professional developmental journey of clinical practice and continuous learning. Are you ready now? If you are like me, when faced with something new, you feel a little nervous. Sure, you just reassured yourself by reviewing the long litany of things you learned in each chapter, but what if . . . ?

-What if no one shows up for group? (What if they do!)
-What if the group gets out of control?
-What if there is too much to do?
-What if the change process backfires?

The rest of this chapter is about anxiety — why it is natural to feel anxious, what the feeling means in relation to group leadership, particularly Directive Group, and what you can do about it. Psychoanalytic and developmental theory coupled with my personal experience will be used to explore these concerns.

Living with Anxiety

Everyone has to deal with anxiety. Everyone — doctors, staff, patients, families, friends — every living person from the psychotic and drugged out to the corporate executive and mother of five. By anxiety I mean the fear of the future, the feeling of dread about what might happen, the clutching misgivings about the past, the sweaty pits, cold hands, rapid pulse, worried face, queasy stomach.

Although everyone has anxiety, everyone experiences it in a different way. Some people aren't as aware of it because they call it something else, like depression, being on edge, or loneliness. But anxiety is part of the human experience, a by-product of living in complex times with multiple choices.

On one level, anxiety is the result of conflicting tendencies to want mutually exclusive needs met simultaneously, for example, fearing and wishing for intimacy and autonomy. At another level, anxiety is the result of unresolved problems from the past. Anxiety can be a signal that danger is about to occur, be the threat real or perceived. Anxiety can also be a response to reality not living up to expectations, be they conscious or unacknowledged.

Over the years, several core issues have repeatedly emerged through my discussions with students, co-leaders, and colleagues: fears of incompetence, perfectionistic strivings, and counter-transference issues. While these are not exhaustive or mutually exclusive, they provide a chance to look at anxiety in relation to Directive Group and your role as a developing therapist.

Anxiety is common when leading groups. The patients pose conflicting demands for your attention and you can't meet them all. The patients evoke ambivalent feelings in you because they have needs and you want to help, but they may also elicit private emotions which you know not to share. Leaders may feel disgust at some patients' appearance, discouragement about how slowly they make progress, or alarm by the extreme impairment that they witness.

It is important to acknowledge these internal experiences as part of the complexity of being in a therapeutic relationship. By tolerating the anxiety from "unacceptable" feelings and exploring their relevance to the treatment process, you become a more highly sensitive instrument of change. Drawing on your knowledge base and clinical experience, you can integrate the many sources of information you have about the patients to further the goals of the group.

Many of the facets of Directive Group are designed to help both you and the patients manage anxiety. The patients cannot afford to experience additional anxiety from being in an uncontrolled, overwhelming situation. Neither do they grow from being in a too tightly controlled one which doesn't allow for some degree of autonomy and spontaneity. Fortunately, the sequence of events, the use of activities which are optimally arousing, the reliance on reasonable short-term goals, and the roles of the co-leaders assist in this regard.

As health professionals, you have a responsibility to know yourself as well as possible. You can't really share a patient's pain, joy, anger, or triumph unless you have owned those parts of yourself. It's also hard to have realistic expectations for patients in your groups if you haven't confronted your own resistance to change. One way to offer patients more authentic help is to engage in your own therapeutic work.

To the extent anxiety interferes with your ability to be an effective group leader, you may want to examine your anxiety to learn what it is telling you. Through accepting, yet honest self-reflection and discussion with a supervisor, friend, or therapist, you can learn to use anxiety as an aid to personal growth. Even though talking about feelings doesn't necessarily get rid of them, it does offer relief and an opportunity for support. Facing feelings is a first step towards healing and changing.

Fears of Incompetence

One common fear of new group leaders is that they aren't doing things right. In Directive Group they may worry that they will plan an activity that won't work, or that what they say to a patient will make him or her worse, or that the co-leader will think they are doing too much or too little, or that they don't really know how to assess the patients' progress, or that they won't be able to lead and observe and coordinate everything at the same time.

Every time you do new things, you are reminded on some emotional level of earlier times when learning something new. Even if you can't remember the specifics, the feelings from the unfinished business remain. If you learned rather easily and successfully, you probably have less current anxiety about failing than if you had more pressured or uneven experiences. But everyone has to deal with the ambiguity of how things will turn out just because no one can guarantee the outcome.

Irrational thoughts are just that: they don't make sense logically. But their presence means they do make sense to those parts of our minds that are still childish. The trick is to discover the meaning they once had and then to use our adult judgment to re-evaluate their relevance for the present. Usually, when seen in the light of day, these old ideas lose their power over us.

Whatever the underlying sources, often a little perspective from others really helps. Ask for specific feedback from your co-therapist on how you lead the group. Part of your problem may be from undervaluing your own skills. You know, if it's easy, it doesn't count. Another problem may be from making the erroneous assumption that you are the only one who struggles. Gathering information from people you trust about how they learned to develop confidence and tolerate mistakes may be illuminating.

Most of all, take a long hard look at yourself. Catalogue your skills and knowledge about adapting activities, understanding psychiatric problems, assessing functional levels of behavior, using effective communication patterns, and following documentation procedures. Identify gaps, then plan which ones to fill in first. Give yourself time to learn. The road to self-discovery and competency is just that — a path, not a destination.

Perfectionistic Strivings

Related to fears of incompetency are perfectionistic strivings. Often individuals with low self-esteem attempt to maintain emotional control by over-controlling things and people around them. Perfectionism is a problem for Directive Group in much the same way that the the extreme pursuit of unrealistic standards affects performance in any area. Energy is wasted, virtues are turned into hindrances, and emotional availability and authenticity are limited.

These present particular problems in Directive Group when the leaders get too hung up with selecting "perfect" activities or goals, or get too critical of each other for "imperfect" interventions. When perfectionism interferes with hearing needed feedback in a nondefensive way, the collaboration necessary for the group is jeopardized. Similarly, it's hard for co-leaders to enjoy knowing each other, let alone "create a playful context" together, when a leader is preoccuried with proving him or herself.

Patients suffer to the extent that their needs are obscured by the personal needs of the leaders. When leaders have unrealistically high expectations for themselves, they tend to expect too much from patients as well. Unknowingly, they set themselves and the patients up for failure. Giving up this pattern is often quite challenging.

Perfectionism can be crippling. First, it's insidious. You may be so busy trying to be perfect that you don't realize how hard you are being on yourself — and others. Then, it is easy to attack perfectionism with the same attitudes that trip you up in the first place. You go after traces of perfectionism with a vengeance. You get more intense trying to rout it out of your life. You are not really changing at all. If anything, you are adding more of the same.

You probably have this problem if:

-You always think you have too much to do and not enough time to do it because you can't do everything to your satisfaction.

-You feel very constrained by the fact of being evaluated by your supervisor because you imagine your supervisor will judge you by the harsh standards to which you hold yourself.

-You read lots of books and do excessive amounts of work at home because you believe there is a right way out there if only you could find it.

-You feel better leading a group alone, as when your co-leader is on vacation, because then you can be more your real self and not get overly anxious when you think you made a mistake or tried to experiment a little.

-You procrastinate or sometimes underprepare for the group activities and goal setting because you are afraid you'll disappoint yourself if you give it your all.

It is important to distinguish the pursuit of excellence from perfection. Excellence is related to high standards, but, unlike perfectionistic standards, a commitment to excellence is attainable given the time, money, and resources available.

Rather than put all your energy into trying to do a perfect job, think through what is necessary to do a terrific job and then move on to something else. It's the old law of diminishing returns. The last 20 percent of your effort is much better spent networking, marketing, politicking, or even playing, than it is polishing something that won't shine that much brighter anyway. You are probably wasting energy hoping you will receive recognition, instead of putting yourself in a position to be noticed and to connect with people who count.

One way out of perfectionism is to convince yourself there really is no one right way. I noticed this graphically when I was teaching. I'd give 25 students an assignment and I would get back 25 different approaches. I would be amazed because I never could have imagined such variety myself, and there were so many reasonable alternatives to the same problem. This type of awareness makes delegating much easier.

The most convincing approach is to get truly fed up with making problems for yourself. Most people don't really change without a significant emotional experience. That is why many short-term treatments are useful for patients. They come after the patient has been significantly stressed and is more open to possibilities than usual. The same may be true for you. It's when you get good and tired of "waiting until" you are perfect to do what you really want to do, that you'll start learning how to use the capacities you DO have in a more adaptive way.

The best way to start meeting your expectations is to lower them. It sounds blasphemous to the uninitiated, or at least like cheating. But I have found the most useful antidote to action paralysis is to ask myself "what CAN I do?" If I can't finish this book by the weekend, can I finish a first draft of a chapter? If you can't write all your progress notes to your specifications, can you write a few thorough ones and do an adequate job on the rest? If you are too tired to cook the gourmet meal you intended for your friends, can you order out pizza or ask them to pitch in?

Try to isolate the areas in which you have the most trouble and experiment with strategies to see what helps your particular brand of perfectionism. If you chronically underestimate time needed to do a project, try planning for two to three times the amount right from the start. If you have trouble setting priorities, try dividing your list of things to do into three piles — must do now, should do soon, and would be nice to do some time. Not every task is worth "achievement level" performance. Try being "only competent" on less crucial activities.

Use your insights about the nature of your problem and your preferred ways of working on your issues before selecting strategies to try. Techniques, like ill-timed interpretations, don't do anything if you aren't ready. Listen to your inner voice. The ironic part about giving up trying so hard, is that you have more energy, are less intense, and end up doing more of what you really want to do anyway. For perfectionists, less is truly more.

Counter-transference

Transference occurs when patients treat you as if you were someone from their past. The process is unconscious and requires considerable therapeutic skill to realize what is happening and how to deal with it sensitively and helpfully. Similarly, being human, sometimes group leaders experience counter-transference and treat a patient or co-leader as someone else. The defense mechanism of projection allows you to unconsciously ascribe to others personally unacceptable impulses, feelings, and thoughts. This can also occur at a group level where the group dynamics elicit from you unconscious material.

How do you become aware of counter-transference when it's happening and deal with it? First, look at the situation as objectively as possible, then explore the remaining irrational thoughts. Remember the adage for psychiatric diagnosing, "rule out the physical first?" Well in this case, rule out the *rational* first so that you can more clearly see your personal issues and make sense of them. Also, give yourself credit for some reality testing through your intuitive senses. You must be picking up something in the air, even if you can't identify it yet.

Let's say you are in Directive Group, feeling anxious, and not sure if your concerns are warranted or counter-transference, but you keep wondering what you would do if the group got out of control. Well, what do you mean, "out of control?" Not cooperating? Yelling? Running out of the room? Having an orgy? Killing someone? I mean, how bad is bad in your mind?!

Directive Group patients sometimes are scary. If they are psychotic, they often don't make sense. Their thoughts, feelings, and behaviors are very disturbed. They have overwhelming anxiety, which you, being sensitive, may pick up on. Even though very few patients in the group in my experience have been physically aggressive, the fear is still realistic. That is why, as we discussed in earlier chapters, attention is given to setting boundaries for them, both concrete and psychological.

For this level of patient the therapeutic task is to help contain their anxiety and "push back" their projections. By way of contrast, if a group leader were to undergo individual psychoanalysis for his or her own self-development, the therapeutic task initially might be to heighten awareness of anxiety and let out the "craziness" through free associating and dream work. The point is that psychotic patients have a way of showing "normal" individuals some of the evil that lurks within. They trigger on an unconscious level the recognition of parts of self-understanding which are hidden, yet perhaps beginning to surface. In reaction to perceiving the potential of aggressive behavior in the group, the group leader may wonder subconsciously, "what impulses am I afraid to acknowledge in myself that could make me feel out of control?"

The answer is not necessarily to run out and get your head examined. Admit the feelings, think about what meaning they may have for you unrelated to the group, and then plan what to do to manage the group therapeutically. For instance, do you know what you would do if someone DID get out of control? You should work out a strategy with your co-leader. You should know the unit's policies on dealing with aggressive behavior and how to use the range of security procedures. You should sharpen your skills on predicting and controlling aggressive behavior.

Fear of aggression isn't the only counter-transference issue in Directive Group. The patients can also arouse intense frustration, impatience, and anger. Some groups are so passive and immobilized, you may feel the impulse to scream, fall asleep, or leave the room. Once, the psychiatrist co-leader and I were at our wits end in such a group and we actually lay down in the middle of the floor to see if our mirroring them would get the patients to move. It didn't. During the post-group we acknowledged we had feelings we weren't admitting and started to deal with them more fully. Only after this process of self-exploration, were we able to problem-solve more effective approaches to use during the group.

Another issue for co-leaders is when their own passivity gets hooked during group sessions. In some ways, the student role evokes passive compliance. During internship you are in a transition period to becoming an active professional. You may not feel totally comfortable sharing with a team what you observed in group, especially when they don't ask your opinion and you have to take the initiative to offer what you know. In the group it is easy to hide behind the more experienced leaders and then, when it is your turn to lead, structure everything to the nth degree to control your anxiety and the group. This is a common pitfall of new group leaders. You need to find a way to work past your urge to be passive without going to the opposite extreme.

All of us are susceptible to the human frailty of acting-out unacknowledged hostility. For example, I have also seen group leaders in residency training who were rigid and punitive with the Directive Group patients. Sometimes, instead of using supportive interactions, they intervened by interpreting patient behavior. Interpretations clearly raise the anxiety of Directive Group patients past what they can tolerate. The trainees know this intellectually because it is discussed in their ongoing supervision. Therefore, the possibility of their acting-out unacknowledged hostility has to be addressed or the patients suffer.

Where to Go from Here

The purpose of this chapter is to emphasize the value in knowing yourself better. One thing we know for sure, wherever you go, you'll be taking that person with you. As you experience the mixed emotions that accompany therapeutic work, you offer yourself and others permission to grow. The more you can appreciate your own complexities, the more you can respond to your patients in genuinely helpful ways. Part of this developmental journey involves:

-Accepting the fact that anxiety is part of human existence — not denying it or becoming paralyzed by it;

-Tolerating the experience of anxiety — rather than acting it out;

-Admitting ambivalent feelings — not hiding from your dark side;

-Owning your personal history — but not being a slave to it;

-Letting go of old patterns — and not taking yourself too seriously.

Returning to our chart on commitment to learning and change, where are you now? You have probably learned the mechanics of leading Directive Group, and now might be the time to practice. Gaining clinical experience is a daily opportunity for fun and self-discovery. Remember the exploratory level of arousal and let yourself "play" with the concepts and techniques for awhile. Get familiar with the activities in the Appendix and learn to trust your judgment on what works for you and your setting. As with learning to cook, this is the time to try recipe after recipe. Throw out the ingredients that don't serve your purposes. Let your senses guide you.

After awhile, you'll find leading the group routinely is a piece of cake. Follow your instincts for those creative flashes and cook up a storm. Now that you are at a competency level regarding this group, enjoy the satisfaction that comes with mastery. Other challenges will present themselves and engage your interest. Your colleagues will see you as a valuable resource and present opportunities for collaboration.

If you want to operate at the achievement level of arousal, go for it. Monitor your priorities so that you have energy for what YOU consider worth this amount of effort and attention. You are innovating now — a two-star gourmet cook. Your knowledge, skills, and experience are at your finger tips to apply to whatever your creativity imagines. You aren't afraid to throw out whole meals sometimes, because you have your vision on quality and are trusting your internal process to guide you.

By learning to be a group leader, you have expanded your identity as a therapist and your commitment to a helping profession. Through developing your program, you have created connections with people, ideas, and processes. These are elements of lifelong learning that are available each day for your renewal and celebration. Bon appetit!

Suggested Reading

Individual Change Processes

Bridges, W. (1983). Transitions. Reading, MA: Addison Wesley.

Clance, P. (1985). The Imposter Phenomenon. Atlanta: Peachtree.

Gawain, S. (1986). Living in the Light. Mill Valley, CA: Whatever Publishers.

Gendlin, E. (1981). Focusing. New York Bantam Books.

Jersild, A. (1955). When Teachers Face Themselves. New York: Teachers College Press.

Jung, C. (1971). The Portable Jung. Campbell, J. (Ed.). New York: Viking Press.

Kaplan, K. (Spring 1987) How I finally lost weight. Whirlpool, Vol. 10, No 1., pp. 20-23.

Sher, B. (1979). Wishcraft: How to Get What You Really Want. New York: Ballantine Books.

Watzlawick, P., Weakland, C., Frisch, R. (1974). Change: Principles of Problem Formation and Problem Resolution. New York: W.W. Norton.

Wheelis, A. (1973). How People Change. New York: Harper & Row.

Psychoanalytic Theory

Brenner C. (1974). An Elementary Textbook of Psychoanalysis. New York: Anchor Books.

Freud, S. (1975). Group Psychology and the Analysis of the Ego. Strachey, J. (Ed.). New York: W.W. Norton.

Missildine, H. (1963). Your Inner Child of the Past. New York: Simon & Schuster.

Viorst, J. (1986). Necessary Losses: The Loves Illusions, Dependencies and Impossible Expectations That All of Us Have to Give Up in Order to Grow. New York: Fawcett Gold Medal.

APPENDIX

This appendix contains a compiled list of 131 activity ideas, descriptions of 69 activities, and a list of 56 of the described activities (Appendix A-2 and A-3) analyzed for quick reference according to the group's energy level, the primary skills required, the needs met, and the necessary preparation.

Compiled List of Directive Group Activities — 131 Ideas

The following activities are the most common and successful activities used with the minimally functioning patients in our short-term setting. They have been developed for use in the group by many staff and student co-leaders over the years.

Like favorite recipes that get passed around to families and friends, the original creator or source of inspiration often gets lost in the shuffle. But sharing good ideas means that that many more people can cook interestingly and eat well. So too with these activities. Even though credit cannot be given where due, the contribution to the many patients who have learned and grown through these activities is immense. May everyone who has ever made up an activity take pleasure in this.

I invite you to continue the process by using these activities as prototypes for adaptations and your own creations. When I plan dinner, I often look through cook books for ideas, not so much for recipes. I may wonder what I can do with the eggplant I bought, and then end up combining what I like from several different recipes to match the ingredients I already have and the tastes I had in mind.

After a while, the experienced Directive Group leader can use these activities in the same way. The activities appropriate for the Directive Group are infinite. The art is in presenting them skillfully, respectfully, and in a therapeutic context.

The compiled list can be referred to as a quick brainstorming tool when planning sessions. We used to list the activities on large poster boards in our co-leaders' meeting room to jog our memories. The chapter is noted when the activity is referred to in the text.

The activities are basically (1) organized by the typical Directive Group sequence of events during a session, and (2) graded within each category in increasing complexity.

Orientation

Fill in the blanks (Chapter 4)
Change arrow on calendar (see monthly calendar description)
Write date, time of group, and name of group on blackboard (Chapter 8)
Show list of ten goals for group (Chapter 6)
Ask old members to explain to new members what is done in Directive Group and why (Chapter 8)
Discuss briefly (Chapter 4):
-What patients did last night
-What patients did over weekend
-What they did over holiday
-What they will do after group
-One thing they will do during weekend
-Who got to the group on time; punctuality issues outside of hospital

Introductions

Balloon (Chapter 4)
Movements
-Throw and catch
-Throw with one bounce
-Keep in the air
-Hit over heads
-Volley using different body parts
Categories
-Names
-Numbers
-Colors
-States
-Sports
-Clothes
-Foods
-Cars
-Holiday items
-Staff member names
-Famous people
-Presidents
-Athletes
-Clothes designers
-Music groups
-Movie titles
-Books
-Artists
-Personal hobbies

-Good places to vacation

Names
Leaders welcome each member by name
Write own name on name tag
Patients pick a prewritten name tag and give it to correct person
Introduce person on left to person on right

Warm-up Activities

Exercises
Imitate leader (Chapter 8)
Move one finger, then increase (Chapter 8)
Each person leads a simple movement, one at a time (Chapter 4)
Lead one exercise at a time following a sequence from toe to head or vice versa
Exercise cards
Stand up exercises
Voice exercises
Demonstrate two movements each time
Body part game
Explain exercise, partner demonstrates
Change movements in sequence (modified game of Concentration)
Hold hands in circle and do simple dance step (step-kick, step-kick)
Hokey Pokey
Simon Says, or (your name) says
Touch and name three body parts in a row

Selected Activities

Parachute Activities
Lean back and pull tight
Pull to left, to right
Hold on lap, move to floor, to lap, to air, reverse and repeat
Waves: light, hard
Bounce Nerf balls; keep on
Bounce Nerf balls; bounce off
Get ball to drop through hole in middle of parachute
Have large ball go around perimeter clockwise
Raise, and two people change places (by names, numbers, color of clothes, people wearing watches)
Walk on parachute
Stand in center, wrap person up (use clinical judgment as to when appropriate)

Sensory Awareness
Color match
Smell bottles, visual bottles

Feely box
Obstacle course
Music: percussion band
Jigsaw puzzles (individual, teams, and group)

Food
Bring in prepared cupcakes
Make, slice, and bake cookies
Make trail mix
Plan a breakfast and eat it together (cereal, fruit, milk, juice)
Make a fruit salad

Active games (using body only, a ball, and familiar objects).
Sit down soccer
Wastebasket basketball
Balloon volleyball
Modified bowling
Relays
Fruit ball
Pass it on
Table soccer
Musical chairs
Back to back
Fruit basket (Chapter 8)
Ring toss (Ring around the bottle)
Bean bag toss
Velcro darts
Tic tac toe
Dodge ball
Hide and seek
Shoe scramble
Marble hide
Suitcase game
Magazine match

Cognitive Games (Communication/Interaction Skills).
Alphabet game, categories
I see (I spy)
Whisper down the lane
Dominoes (giant size)
Opposite cards
Hangman
Facts of three (or five)
Chinese checkers
Magazine scavenger hunt
Cards (Black Jack, Old Maid, Uno)
Going on a trip
Pass the can (modified charades)

Crafts

Bead necklaces
Adult designs to color
Teapot memo pad
Mugs to decorate
Decoupage plaques or key chains
Leather stamping key chains
Copper tooling coaster
Tissue paper flowers
Mobile: gods' eyes or wind chimes
Block printing greeting cards
Sand terrariums (Chapter 8)
Monthly calendar
Mural (collage wall hanging)

Wrap-up

List activities of session, raise hand for one liked the best
Vote on activities liked, would do again, were the hardest
Good, Better, Best
Guess what
Guess who
Which skills
Individual goals
Graduation awards/certificates of participation

Descriptions of 69 Activities

Activities are described in four main sections:

-A general purpose stating how the main component of the activity contributes to the goals of the group

-The materials needed to set up the activity

-The usual process for doing the activity. The basic conceptualization provides the model for further adaptations. Co-leaders need to take care when explaining the name of a game or the instructions to use only non-provocative and easy to understand language.

-Adaptations suggesting other activity ideas or ways to increase or decrease the complexity, novelty, or uncertainty of the presentation. Adaptations require that the co-leaders analyze the cognitive and group interaction levels within the group, and match the activity accordingly.

The *orientation* activities are combined into one, since they take a short amount of time and rely on similar written and oral processes. They are designed to help the group know where they are and what to expect.

The *introduction* activities include balloon games and other ways to introduce members to the group. The balloon games are highly adaptable and often become part of the warm-up activities. They can emphasize the movement component as well as cognitive challenges. The name activities are more verbal and cognitive and can be graded according the level of group skill and cohesiveness.

The **warm-up** activities are simple movement exercises and games. They are very much geared to the energy level of the group and are highly adaptable. They require little advance preparation, so they lend themselves to adapting on the spot.

The **selected activities** include the widest range of options — parachute activities, active games, verbal games, crafts, sensory awareness, and food activities.

Parachute activities are excellent for increasing the energy level of passive groups and channeling the energy level of hyperactive or negative groups. They can be adapted to allow more organized patients to take a role initiating ideas.

Sensory awareness activities are used mostly with groups with low energy, patients with depression and organicity, and some cohesiveness. They often require substantial preparation, so they are not good when trying to incorporate new patients. The activities provide basic cognitive and perceptual challenges and stimulation. They are used, like the other activities, for their potential for meeting the needs of the group and eliciting behavior toward the group goals. Although behavioral observation may reveal individual patient problems in this area, the group is not attempting to provide neurologically based treatment.

Food-related activities are used sparingly. They are tied to the emotional needs of the group. Often patients in Directive Group seem to resist nurturing through oral gratification. When the group initiates interest in food it is followed up by the leaders. Food activities take substantial preparation but have many opportunities for grading them (e.g., from just eating, to preparation at a parallel level, to the level of parts to the whole).

Active games use the body only, ball activities, or familiar objects. They are helpful in promoting participation and spontaneous interaction. They are not taxing verbally or cognitively, but they can be adapted to allow for more challenge in these areas for individual patients within the group structure.

Cognitive games are used before the wrap-up. After the group has been stimulated through their motor skills, they are more able to concentrate on cognitive tasks. The activities are generally verbal and calming, and help to prepare for transition to the end of the group and return to the unit. Some of the activities are more active and require social interaction as part of the game.

Crafts are generally used when the group can tolerate a longer activity, although not past one group session. They are often set up as a parallel activity with little interaction expected at this point and attention to the task emphasized. At the same time, there are opportunities for some sharing and for more verbal patients to feel comfortable interacting. Sometimes the crafts are structured as a group activity in which each person's part contributes to the whole. Opportunities for more organized patients to be more creative or helpful to others are frequent. Almost all craft sessions include a structured discussion about the experience.

Wrap-up activities help the group review the processes of the session and bring a sense of closure. Patients pull up their chairs facing the blackboard. The activities are highly adaptable and, since they require little advance preparation, rely greatly on the co-leaders for what would be the most useful way to connect with the patients. The co-leaders have to be attentive to who is new in the group, who is leaving, and who is working on which goals. They give and solicit feedback during this phase, and their warmth and skill in conducting this part is very important.

Orientation Activities

Purpose: To make sure patients are oriented to person, place, and time.

Materials: Blackboard and chalk, arrow and monthly calendar, poster of ten goals.

Process: Have patients fill in blanks on blackboard about name of group, date, and purpose of group. Have one patient change the arrow on the large monthly calendar to the correct day.

Adaptations: Add complexity by having patients write information on the blackboard with verbal cues, but not fill in the blank. Have brief discussions about goals (of group), plans (e.g., what you did last night), or values (e.g.,punctuality). Varying the topics adds novelty.

Introduction Activities

Balloon Activities

Purpose: To capture attention of group through a motor response. To learn names and see self as part of a group.

Materials: Large red balloon. $1.50 each from Red Balloon, 1073 Wisconsin Avenue, Washington, D.C. 20007, (202) 965-9394; inflator from Equipment Shop, Box 33, Bedford, MA 01730.

Process: Throw balloon to a group member, all of whom are seated in a circle, and say his or her name. Each member throws balloon to another until everyone has had at least one throw. If person doesn't know a name, he or she is encouraged to ask.

Adaptations: If group is movement-oriented, focus on keeping balloon in air, bouncing it, or hitting it with various body parts. Often co-leaders make jokes, such as when a person hits the balloon with his head: "Now that's what I call using your head!"

If the group needs novelty, add categories while throwing the balloon (e.g., cars, states, famous people). Complexity is added by difficulty of category and length of time exhausting it.

Names

Purpose: For each person to know who is in the group and to feel valued as an individual member.

Materials: Name tags and markers.

Process: Have patients fill out name tags. When each person is done, they say their names.

Adaptations: Fill out name tags before group. Let patients pick a name tag and give it to the person it belongs to.

For a relatively organized group, have patient on left introduce patient on right.

Warm-up Activities

Exercises

Purpose: To engage patients interest and attention through basic body movement. To allow for feelings of groupness without stress of verbal interaction. To encourage simple rule behaviors, like taking turns and delaying immediate gratification.

Materials: Chairs in a circle, floor space adequate to move around. (Body Awareness Cards from Trend Enterprises, St. Paul, MN 55164)

Process: Leaders ask one person at a time, in sequence, to demonstrate a movement. The group imitates that person.

Adaptations: Novelty provided through altering order of exercises (e.g., head to toe) or using different exercises (e.g., voice exercises: "Say 'loud' real loud"; Body Awareness Cards: patients do the motion pictured on the card).

Complexity is added by playing movement games (e.g., Simon Says or Hokey Pokey), increasing number of movements (e.g., two movements each time, touch and name three body parts in a row), standing up (e.g., have one person explain a movement, have the partner demonstrate it to the group), or teaching a dance step (holding hands, step on the right foot, kick with the left, reverse, repeat step, kick, step, kick, then expand with claps, walking, turning, etc.).

Uncertainty can be decreased by having patients imitate leader who starts with fingers and moves slowly in sequence from head to toe.

Modified Concentration

Purpose: To increase challenge of movement activities. Add demands for increased concentration, initiation, and coordination.

Materials: Seated in circle.

Process: One person starts a repetitive movement (e.g., clapping hands) and others follow. Then next person leads. Perhaps they hit both thighs with their palms.

Adaptations: Have each person repeat the movement done previously, then add the new one.

Complexity is added by leading three movements in a row.

Uncertainty is increased by having one patient leave the room briefly while a leader is picked. When he or she comes back, the movements are in progress. The patients try to follow the leader's movements quickly so that it is harder for that patient to guess who the leader is.

Body Part Game

Purpose: To enhance memory, body awareness, and basic interaction through movement.

Materials: Chairs in a circle.

Process: Each person picks a body part and tells it to the group. The designated leader points to his or her chosen body part and says it out loud, then points to the body part of another group member and says it out loud. Then that person is the leader and continues the process.

Precautions: Could be provocative with certain groups. Co-leaders can role-model how to play and use judgment when to quit.

Selected Activities

Parachute Activities

Purpose: To increase energy level, attention, and interaction of the group through stimulating and nonthreatening movements with an object.

Materials: Parachute may be purchased from army surplus stores or catalog. Nerf balls of assorted sizes and colors. A beach ball.

Process: Start with patients sitting in a circle, each holding the outside rim of the parachute with both hands. Ask group to make waves gently, then harder.

Adaptations: The parachute adds novelty to the group activities because of its uncommon use in daily activities. The novelty can be further increased by the many variations possible:

-If the group is low energy, start with pulling back so the parachute is tight. Then lean right and then left. Repeat until group seems comfortable but not bored.

-Another slow movement is to have group touch parachute to floor (by bending forward in their chairs), then touch their lap, then reach up high. Then go to making waves. If necessary, all the activities can be done from chairs, but usually the group is ready to stand for the following activities.

-Complexity can be increased by adding Nerf balls. Instruct group to bounce the balloons on the parachute but not to let them go off. This usually gets people laughing because a few bounce off. Then say, "Now, let's get all of them off." More laughter and energy.

-A beach ball can be used to go around the outside perimeter of the parachute. Requires group cooperation and coordination, allowing for more organized patients to take initiative through developing their role in the group. On some parachutes there is a hole in the center which the beach ball can go through as another challenge.

-Uncertainty can be increased by asking people to trade places. The group counts to three and raises hands so people can go under the parachute. Identify people by names, numbers (as many as in group or ones, twos, and threes), everyone wearing a watch or glasses, and so forth. For instance, "Everyone wearing something red change places." The co-leaders have to pick these carefully so there won't be chaos, unless it would be funny to end by having controlled chaos; with some groups this is just right.

-Sometimes patients like to walk on the waves. Group holds the parachute low to the ground and person walks around slowly. Make sure person has good balance. Other times a patient can stand in the center and the group wraps him or her up by raising their arms and they circle around. Usually people volunteer who feel comfortable with this much attention. Use clinical judgment to monitor and don't push anyone to do anything.

Sensory Awareness

Color Match

Purpose: To increase attention and interaction through game requiring visual discrimination and speed.

Materials: Thirty 5 × 7 pieces of colored construction paper (five different colors) and five 8 × 10 colored pieces of construction paper. Large table and chairs.

Process: Place the large pieces of paper in the center of the table. Mix up all the colors of the small cards and deal them to each patient in turn until the pile is gone. Group members are asked to match the small cards with the large cards by placing them on the large cards as fast as possible when the leader says Go.

Sensory Awareness Day

Purpose: Use activities which increase awareness of the five senses to stimulate attention, interests, and interaction.

Materials: Clear plastic bottles containing salt, sugar, and flour (several of each); same and different cards (Developmental Learning Materials Catalog),* fragrance bottles, feely box (cardboard box with a hole on the side, filled with common items such as a pipe cleaner, emery board, feather, eraser, sandpaper, paper clip, and a cup), and an obstacle course (use chairs and tables to create path. Draw arrows or write simple instructions on about five individual large index cards).

Process: Set up four stations around the room with simple procedural instructions at each station (written on large paper). Patients are divided into four subgroups and rotate through each station accompanied by a co-leader (or staff or student visitor who was prepared for his or her role prior to the group).

1. Visual discrimination station. Ask patients to look at the same and different cards and match them. Then ask them to match the substances in the clear bottles containing salt, sugar, or flour.

2. Olfactory discrimination station. Ask patients to identify the smells in each of the bottles. May use spices, cologne, strong foods, and so forth. (Some stores sell scents in bottles.)

3. Use feely box for tactile discrimination. Ask patients to feel one object at a time in the box and say what it is without looking.

4. Set up obstacle course for motor planning and following written directions. Use arrows to show direction to walk. Then have patients do movements such as turn left, step up, jump down, turnaround, and walk backwards.

Adaptations: Set up a station for auditory discrimination using opaque containers with objects in them to shake. Ask them to say what it sounds like, guess what might be in them, or ask them to identify which one has the rice, marbles, or whatever in them.

Use the obstacle course as a separate selected activity on a given day. After the first obstacle course is set up by the leaders, have the more organized patients help set up other ones. Bring in extra cards and markers to show the way. While the group is setting up, the other patients can watch, help, or be involved with a co-leader in a quick game of Nerf ball catch or hangman. Co-leaders can assess how to use time to adapt on the spot.

Percussion Band

Purpose: To encourage attention and participation through musical stimulation.

*DLM Teaching Resources, P.O. Box 4000, 1OLM Park, Allen, TX 75002.

Materials: Assorted percussive instruments. Patients seated in a circle.

Process: Have instruments out on middle of floor. Each person selects one. Everyone tries his or hers all at the same time. Then go around circle and have each person play. Then do it all together again. Can divide group in half and have them take turns. Then have patients trade instruments and repeat.

Adaptations: Can play music on tape recorder and have patients accompany it rhythmically. Can play equivalent of body part game, using an instrument to identify self, by name and by playing it, and then calling on the next person to do the same.

Jigsaw Puzzles

Purpose: To increase concentration, encourage cooperation (or beginning competition), and match low energy level with perceptually challenging activity.

Materials: 50-to 100-piece large jigsaw puzzles available at some toy stores or variety stores. Look for adult themes, like pictures of animals, houses, or scenery. (Individual blank 12-and 28-piece puzzles available from S&S Crafts Catalog, Colchester, CT 06145.)

Process: Jigsaw pieces are placed picture side up on a table. Patients are shown the completed picture on the top of the box. Patients gather round to work on puzzle. Good for smaller group, or can have several puzzles with a co-leader with each subgroup.

During group or wrap-up the discussion may naturally turn to personal hobbies (since jigsaws are a common adult leisure activity) or issues like not finishing (although 50 pieces is about right for most groups).

Adaptations: Use as a parallel activity with smaller puzzles. Patients can design puzzles by tracing designs, painting, or drawing with markers. Then take the pieces apart and reassemble. Play Dueling Jigsaws in which two teams get the same jigsaw puzzle. See which team completes the puzzle first.

Food Activities

Cupcakes

Purpose: To express caring for members and emphasize separate identities symbolically through food. To create rituals for celebrations of birthdays and holidays.

Materials: Co-leaders bring in enough cupcakes (or muffins or doughnuts or whatever) for each person to have one. Bring napkins, juice, and cups, if desired.

Process: Each person is encouraged to take one item to eat. May want to sing Happy Birthday or other songs and briefly discuss the event.

Slice and Bake Cookies

Purpose: To prepare food for self and group. To delay gratification by waiting for cookies to bake and cool.

Materials: Cookie sheets, cookie dough, knives, napkins, paper plates, juice, and cups. Need close access to an oven.

Process: In our setting the room for Directive Group is across from the kitchen which makes access very easy. This task is usually set up with division of labor to develop basic role behavior. Some people cut, some arrange on the cookie sheet, some watch the oven and wait for the cookies to be done, some pass out cookies, and all help clean up.

It is good to have other activities to do during the waiting time, such as Facts of Five at the blackboard or table soccer.

Trail Mix

Purpose: To make an individual contribution to a group effort. Often done in connection with a unit function, like a Halloween party.

Materials: Bag of peanuts, bag of raisins, bag of M & Ms, box of granola cereal, and anything else that sounds good. Large bowl, long handled spoon, paper cups, and small decoration cups.

Process: Each patient pours a bag of food into the large bowl. Someone stirs it up. Patients then scoop out a cup of trail mix and pour it into little decoration cups. They can eat some and the rest is placed on trays to contribute to the unit party for that evening.

Discussion often follows naturally about holidays, hiking, or nutrition. Co-leaders encourage expression of interests, plans, and concern for self-care.

Breakfast

Purpose: To acknowledge the importance of the relationships in the group and support the cohesiveness. To build on basic planning skills.

Materials: Individual cereal boxes, milk cartons, juice, plates, cups, silver-ware, napkins, and assorted pieces of fruit.

Process: Based on the patients' plan, the co-leaders either bring in food from the grocery store (i.e., the group meets at 9:30 a.m. and there is petty cash available for group activities — details that allow you to adapt to own situation) or the patients order the breakfast from Dietary the previous night and wait to eat until group. The co-leaders still supplement the trays with food so they will have something to eat, too. Patients set table, eat together, discuss the interactions in the group, and clean up.

Fruit Salad

Purpose: To foster the role relationships which have developed in the group. To encourage planning skills and expression of interests.

Materials: Large assortment of fresh fruit from grocery store, several cutting boards, knives and spoons, colander, bowls, and access to sink.

Process: Patients plan the fruit salad during the wrap-up the previous day and co-leaders bring the supplies. Patients take out the fruit from the grocery bag and distribute it to whoever volunteers to prepare each piece. Fruits are put into the large bowl, mixed, and served in individual bowls.

Patients may discuss what skills were required to do such a joint task, what meaning the activity had for them, and how far they have come in terms of self-direction.

Active Games

Sit Down Soccer

Purpose: To stimulate an active response through kicking a ball and increase interest in what is going on around them.

Materials: A large (7-inch) Nerf ball.

Process: Group members arrange their chairs in a circle with a distance apart just large enough for the Nerf ball to pass through. The object of the game is to score points by kicking the ball between the chairs or under the person's chair. The ball is not kicked above seat level. The defenders try to kick the ball away and make their own points. Emphasis is less on the score and more on the energy level and fun. People are advised to take off clunky shoes.

Adaptations: The game is easily adapted to teams in two lines facing each other, so is very congenial to large groups. Because the game requires almost a reflexive response, it is good to use with new patients. Can be made more complex by adding a second ball.

Wastebasket Basketball

Purpose: To practice gross motor coordination, to provide a physical challenge, and to play a game with rules and structure.

Materials: Wastebasket and Nerf ball.

Process: Each person takes a turn at throwing the ball into a basket. Players may stand or sit, and may choose a shooting distance which is challenging for them. Group may designate number of shots given to each player and scoring.

Adaptations: Keep score by teams.

Balloon Volleyball

Purpose: To encourage active participation in team game, increase feelings of belonging to a specific group, and stimulate motor response.

Materials: A net, masking tape, and large balloon.

Process: Group divides into two teams. The goal is to hit the balloon over the net as many times as possible. Group is encouraged to set it up to each other. Emphasis is on helping each other and the movement experience.

Adaptations: Group can devise a system for scoring, rotating positions, and strategy.

Modified Bowling

Purpose: To engage in a familiar game which requires taking turns and scoring.

Materials: Ten large empty plastic soda bottles, white tape, red tape, soccer or volleyball, chalk, blackboard, and eraser.

Process: Soda bottles are covered with white tape and decorated with a red stripe to resemble bowling pins. (This could be a task group project donated to Directive Group.) Place pins in rows of four-three-two-one. Designate a line from which to roll the ball. Each player gets two turns to knock down all the pins. Write score on board (simplified scoring for strikes and spares).

Adaptations: Play by teams or have a group score so no one feels singled out for not getting a high score. May lead to discussion of sportsmanship or enthusiasm for the game itself during lag time when members wait for their turn.

Relays

Purpose: To use minimal competition to increase the energy level and emotional responsiveness of the group.

Materials: Two small (4-inch) Nerf balls.

Process: Patients are seated in two equal lines with their chairs facing each other. At the count of three, the first person passes the Nerf ball to the next person, continuing down the line. When the last person gets the ball, he or she holds it up in the air. The team that gets the ball to the end first, wins. Adaptations: To add a verbal component and more excitement, the last person to get the ball on one team can sing the verse to a familiar song, such as "Row, Row, Row Your Boat." The team that finishes singing the verse first is the winner.

Novelty can be increased by using different size balls and other shaped objects, such as bean bags. Complexity can be increased by using two or more balls at one time, in sequence. The passing can be increased to going down the line and back before winning.

The type of passing can be changed to include using only the right hand, passing under a leg, going behind the back, or alternating high and low with every other person. A higher energy level can be matched by standing up.

If competition in teams is too threatening, the group as a whole, seated in a circle, can time itself and try to decrease the duration in subsequent relays. Uncertainty can be increased by sitting behind each other and passing the ball, or by telling the members to surprise the next person with the way they pass it.

Fruit Ball

Purpose: To increase energy level, verbal interaction, and initiative within the task. Good for a largely elderly group.

Materials: A large selection of Nerf balls, varying in color and size.

Process: Members sit in a circle and start by passing one ball. The group decides what fruit to call it based on its size and color. For instance, a small red ball may be called "cherry." Every time the ball is passed, each person says the label of the ball (type of fruit). Then another ball is added and a fruit label is given. No matter how many balls are added, each one gets a label which is repeated with each pass.

Adaptations: Complexity can be added by passing the ball in interesting ways along with saying the different fruits; for example, under the legs, over the head, behind the back, and so on.

Uncertainty can be added by surprising the group when another ball is added and in the way it is passed. Patient groups add novelty by the way they label fruits; one group will call green "grape," the next will call it "kiwi."

Pass It On

Purpose: To enhance group interaction through touching and increase the ability to receive, interpret, and repeat physical signals.

Materials: Group holding hands in a circle.

Process: Start with everyone standing in a circle holding hands. One person gives a quick squeeze to the hand of the person on his or her right.

This signal gets passed along to the next person, until the original squeeze is received back again in the first person's left hand. Continue to pass it until squeeze is traveling smoothly around the circle.

Adaptations: Change signal to two squeezes, a wink, a handshake, or other friendly signals. Reverse the action for more fun. Can do sitting as well.

Table Soccer

Purpose: To stimulate an active response through a game which offers challenge through eye-hand coordination. Good for a low energy group.

Materials: Nerf ball, table and chairs.

Process: Members of the group sit around the table(s) and place their palms on the edge. A Nerf ball is in play. The object of the game is to keep the ball in motion on the table top as long as possible.

Adaptations: To increase competition, ask members to try to get the ball off the table while each person tries to block the attempt. To add complexity, use two or more balls at one time.

Musical Chairs

Purpose: To increase energy level, encourage paying attention to auditory cues, and facilitate active participation.

Materials: Chairs in a line, alternating facing one wall and the other wall; music.

Process: There is one less chair than the number of participants. Everyone walks around the line of chairs as the music plays. When the music stops, everyone sits down. The person without a chair is out of the game. Then one more chair is removed. The game ends when one of the last two people sits in the one remaining chair.

Adaptations: To avoid the experience of losing, no one is out of the game and no extra chairs are removed. The fun is in avoiding being the person left standing each time. Associations to childhood are reduced when music matches members' preferences.

Back to Back

Purpose: To increase tolerance of physical contact, facilitate social interaction, and engage in a gross motor game.

Materials: Group standing in an open area.

Process: Members stand facing a partner. One member, without a partner, calls out movements for others to follow, for example, "elbow to elbow, knee to knee, finger to finger." When the person yells "back to back," players switch partners and lock elbows back to back. The caller finds a partner and someone else becomes the caller.

Adaptations: If interlocking elbows back to back is too complex or threatening, members can just stand back to back.

Fruit Basket

Purpose: To increase energy level, encourage listening to directions, and facilitate active participation.

Materials: Chairs in a circle, one less than the number of members.

Process: Members are called "apple," "orange," or "pear." The standing member calls out one of the fruits and people with that label change seats. When "fruit basket" is called, everyone switches seats and a new person becomes the caller.

Adaptations: Other labels can be used, for example, ones, twos, and threes — everybody; Hondas, Chevies, and Volvos — parking lot.

Ring Toss (Ring Around the Bottle)

Purpose: To practice gross motor coordination, play a game requiring taking turns, and encourage active participation.

Materials: Rubber rings and wood stand or bowling pin and embroidery hoops.

Process: The stand is set up at one end of the room. Patients stand a challenging distance away and throw the rings. The object is to have the rings circle the wood dowels or bowling pin.

Adaptations: Each individual can pick a distance which is not too easy and not too hard and which can vary after each turn. Game can be played sitting or standing.

Warm-up shots and several throws (e.g., four rings) at once make each person's turn more likely to be successful. Extra rings help to keep the game moving by not having to wait between every turn to retrieve the rings.

Game can be organized by individual efforts, team efforts, or the group as a whole. Points can be kept for various degrees of closeness to the stand, not just for getting the ring around the wood.

Bean Bag Toss

Purpose: To practice gross motor skills and eye-hand coordination, concentrating on a game, and actively participating in a common task.

Materials: Bean bags and a target.

Process: Arrange the target and have patients throw bean bags at it.

Adaptations: The target can be a "twister board" with four rows of colored circles. The bean bags can be made of the same four colors. The game is made more challenging by not only getting a bean bag on a circle, but by matching the colors.

The target can be a large tic tac toe board (then you have "tic tac toss"). You can throw bean bags in the squares or try to choose x's and o's. The target can be a waste basket, a low dish bucket, a wooden board with holes cut out worth different points, and so on. The game can be structured individually, by teams, or the group as a whole.

Velcro Darts

Purpose: To encourage active participation through a game requiring attention, taking turns, and eye-hand coordination.

Materials: Velcro board and ping pong darts with Velcro strips from DLM catalog.

Process: Members stand at a challenging distance and throw the ping pong darts at the velcro board on the wall.

Adaptations: Individual, team, or group as a whole scoring. Can do from chairs if necessary. Distance, number of chances, and speed of game can be used to vary complexity.

Tic Tac Toe

Purpose: To play a game with rules, active involvement, and strategy.

Materials: Group seated facing blackboard, file cards with x's and o's, masking tape.

Process: Members are divided into two teams (x's and o's). Members on team x each receive a card with an x marked on it; same procedure for team o. A large tic tac toe board is drawn on the blackboard. Players take turns going to the board and taping their card in one of the squares. Teams alternate until one team gets three in a row or no one wins.

Adaptations: Some groups have fun being the x's and o's themselves, with the tic tac toe board marked off with masking tape on the floor. More organized patients can help organize their team, plan strategy, and stand on a chair to keep perspective on the large human board.

Dodge Ball

Purpose: To practice gross motor skills, follow rules of a game, and to actively participate in a common task.

Materials: Nerf balls.

Process: One player stands in middle of circle. Players on the outside of circle roll ball at center player, who attempts to avoid being hit. Play continues as long as center person is successful in dodging ball. When center player is hit, he or she changes places with the person in the circle who rolled the ball.

Adaptations: If one person in the center is too threatening for the group or some of its members, two people can be in the center as partners. When either is hit, both go out. The game can be played with participants seated and center player standing, or with two teams standing (one team throws at other team, then reverse).

Hide and Seek

Purpose: To improve observation skills, enhance active participation, and promote feelings of success.

Materials: Small pieces of individually wrapped hard candy.

Process: One player is selected to leave the room. Another player is asked to hide a piece of candy in the room. The player who left the room tries to find the candy. The group members help the player find the candy by saying "Hot" or "Cold" (or "You're getting warmer," etc.). When the player finds the candy, he or she gets to eat it. This can continue until each player gets to find the candy.

Adaptations: One team could hide several pieces of candy from the other, then reverse. Other items could be hidden, for instance, a patient's shoe, which when found is put on, or a card with an instruction, which when found is read and responded to (using the cards from Pass the Can).

Shoe Scramble

Purpose: To enhance observation and sequencing skills, increase rate of reaction, and encourage active participation.

Materials: Group members' shoes.

Process: Group sits in a circle. All players remove one shoe and place it in the middle of the circle. Each player is then asked to pick a shoe that is not his own. The game begins by having each player pass the shoes to the right until each player receives his or her own shoe, after which the player puts on the shoe. The first player to put on his or her shoe is the winner.

Adaptations: Alternate passing shoe to the right one time, to the left the next. Increase complexity by passing with an overhead or underleg approach. Increase uncertainty by playing with eyes closed.

Marble Hide

Purpose: To increase attention, fine motor coordination, and task-oriented interaction.

Materials: One small marble.

Process: Group members are seated in a circle. One person is designated the detective and turns his or her back to the group. The group members ball both fists and pass a marble around the circle as discreetly as possible. The detective walks around the outside of the ring and gets two tries to guess who has the marble.

Adaptations: Have two people be the detective at once. The group can play the game standing. They can be encouraged to fake passes and add mysterious winks, smiles, and so forth.

Suitcase Game

Purpose: To enhance visual memory, rate of reaction, and eye-hand coordination.

Materials: Stop watch, small suitcase, small objects such as a pencil, pen, tape.

Process: The packed suitcase is passed to each lap of the members. Each group member selects an object from the suitcase. The group leader begins the game by putting his or her object in the suitcase, closing the suitcase and passing it to the person on his or her right. The next person opens the suitcase and repeats the procedure. This is done as fast as possible, timed by the stop watch.

Adaptations: After the first round, the suitcase is passed around and group members take items out, instead, as fast as possible.

A more verbal group can go around the circle and make one comment about their object, such as when they use it, why they chose it, or who else would like it.

Magazine Match

Purpose: To increase speed of eye-hand coordination, to stimulate attention to directions, and encourage verbal response.

Materials: Assortment of magazines.

Process: The group is seated in a circle. Each player selects a magazine. The leader asks the group to find certain items in the magazines. The first one to rip the page out of the magazine and show the item to the group is the designated winner for that round. Suggested items include a book, coat, shoes, trees, a sailboat, a baby, a man, a woman, food, cigarettes, a telephone, a lamp, and flowers.

Adaptations: A more verbal group can go around the circle and discuss something about the items, such as which item they would really enjoy, something they would like to give as a gift, or why something is really important to have.

Cognitive Games

Alphabet Game Categories
Purpose: To foster use of cognitive skills through active participation in a verbal activity.

Materials: Blackboard, chalk, and eraser. Group is seated facing the blackboard.

Process: The group selects on object category (e.g., cars, fruits, states, cities, flowers, famous people, vegetables, etc.). Letters of the alphabet are listed in order on the board. Players name an object of the designated category for each letter of the alphabet.

Adaptations: Players may call out answers one at a time, or at random. May also be played in teams, with teams alternating giving answers.

I See Something (I Spy)
Purpose: To encourage memory, observation, and verbal interaction skills.

Materials: Patients seated around the room.

Process: Leader begins by saying "I see something red." One group member at a time guesses what that might be, for instance, a patient's watch band, the arrow on the calendar, or whatever else is red. When the person guesses correctly, then he or she takes the leader role.

Adaptations: The original game is called I Spy, but the paranoid implications should usually be avoided. The game can be more complex by describing the object instead of naming one characteristic of it. For example, "I see something that is used for keeping track of time" (a stop watch).

Whisper Down the Lane
Purpose: To enhance group interaction through a communication game in which members can practice receiving and relaying a message.

Materials: Pen and note cards.

Process: Members sit in a circle. One person is given a card with a sentence on it. That person whispers the sentence to the next person. Each person relays the message in sequence. The last person to receive the message announces what he or she has heard. (Usually this is a distortion of the original message. After laughing and playing a few rounds, discussion can center on what makes for clear communication and what makes it hard to communicate.)

Adaptations: Message may focus on themes, like holidays, someone's birthday, the upcoming weekend or month. With a large group, the game may be played in two teams, comparing the last two people's announcement of the same message.

Dominoes

Purpose: To focus on visual matching, use of space, and basic movements through a cognitive game.

Materials: Giant-size rubber dominoes.

Process: Group sits in a circle. All of the dominoes are distributed. The first person places one on the floor in the center of the circle. The next person checks to see if any of his or her dominoes matches the number of dots on either end of the original domino. If so, he or she gets up and places the matching end next to the other one. If not, it is the next player's turn. The game continues until all of the dominoes are used up which can match.

Adaptations: The dominoes can be added to one end of the growing chain or to both ends. The shape of the attached dominoes can be varied depending on how the domino is placed, either vertically or horizontally. The game can be played with teams and scoring.

Opposite Cards

Purpose: To encourage verbal interaction through matching opposite concepts.

Materials: Opposite cards from DLM catalog.

Process: Group sits in a circle. All of the cards are distributed. The first player picks a card, places it on the floor in the center of the circle, and asks "Who has the opposite of up?" The player with the down card places it on top. Now that player picks a card and the process continues until all of the cards are used up.

Adaptations: The game can be varied by playing in teams. One team places five cards face up on the table. The other team tries to match as many as they can. Then the original team fills in the rest. Time can be kept and the teams reverse roles. The team to contribute the most cards the quickest wins the round.

Verbal interaction can be increased by discussing the pictures on the cards (e.g., Which do people like better, day or night?), demonstrating the concepts (e.g., showing a movement for up and down), or elaborating on the ideas (e.g., What kind of things do you do during the summer that you don't get to do during the winter?).

Modified Hangman

Purpose: To provide a cognitive challenge, encourage verbal interaction, and increase attention to group experience. When used as a wrap-up, to emphasize roles, themes, and feelings in the group, and to enhance memory and attention to the environment.

Materials: Blackboard, chalk, and eraser. Group is seated facing the blackboard.

Process: Used as a transition from the selected activities to the wrap-up, the leader makes lines on the board for the number of letters in a word. The leader says what category the word is in, such as names of people in the group, the feeling of the group during the session, an activity which was done, clothes patients are wearing, or objects in the room. Participants guess letters. If the letter is in the word, it is written on the blank and the guesser gets another turn. If it is not in the word, the letter gets listed above and the next person gets a turn. This continues until the word is guessed.

Adaptations: Used as a wrap-up, focus may be more on the skills used in the group, the main topic discussed in the group, or roles people took.

A little stick figure can be drawn of a man hanging from a gallows. With each wrong guess, another piece is drawn until the man is "hanged." However, because of the concrete nature of the thought processes of most of the patients in this group and the prevalence of suicidal ideation, this is usually changed to a stick figure without reference to the execution part of the game. If the game is used as a selected activity, many other categories can be used, such as titles to songs, names of countries, and so on.

Facts of Three (or Five)

Purpose: To assess cognitive skills and aid patients in increasing awareness of interests and knowledge. If played in teams, to encourage exploration of roles and awareness of cooperative and competitive aspects of the game.

Materials: Blackboard, chalk, eraser, or individually Xeroxed grid sheets.

Process: Group decides on a three-letter word and three categories of things (see example below). The object of the game is to fill in the entire grid by coming up with words in each category which begin with each letter.

Adaptations: If pressed for time or introducing a particular activity, co-leaders may draw grid and have preselected the word and categories. To make more complex, can select a five-letter word and five categories. Try not to repeat any letters in the given word.

To play the game in teams, use a time limit. At the end, have each team call out their answers one square at a time. Points can be used to increase incentives; for instance, the same answers, 1 point; different answers, 2 points; and blanks, 0 points.

Chinese Checkers

Purpose: To interact through attention to a game of strategy and fine motor coordination (good when group is relatively small, low energy, and cognitively organized).

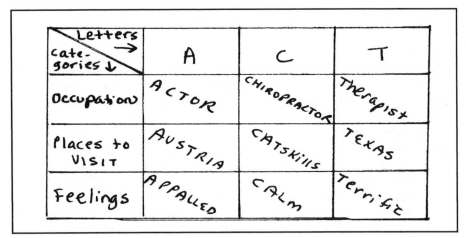

Letters → / Categories ↓	A	C	T
Occupation	ACTOR	CHIROPRACTOR	Therapist
Places to visit	Austria	Catskills	Texas
Feelings	Appalled	Calm	Terrific

Table A-1. Facts of Three

Materials: Chinese checkers board and marbles (one set per six players).

Process: Six players sit around board (if there are more than six members, organize two games simultaneously) and select a color of marbles. Moving clockwise, each person moves one of his or her marbles one space. As more marbles enter the center of the board, players can jump over marbles, as in checkers, only no marbles are removed. The object of the game is to get as many marbles as possible to the point of the star at the opposite side.

Adaptations: The game can be played until people want to do something else, rather than until someone wins. The emphasis is on concentrating, seeing options for moving the marble, and helping each other (a rainy day type of activity).

Magazine Scavenger Hunt

Purpose: To increase simple problem-solving skills, attention to a sequence of visual stimuli, and verbal interactions.

Materials: Pictures from magazines mounted on cardboard and numbered.

Process: Co-leaders hang the pictures around the room. Paper is handed out to each member with clues on them. Members must find the picture that matches each clue and place the number next to the clue. For example, a picture of an apple may have a clue of "fruit."

Adaptations: To be more challenging, add some humor, such as the clue for "apple" may be an obvious picture of New York (the Big Apple). The game can be played individually or in teams.

Black Jack Card Game

Purpose: To encourage interaction and attention through a game of matching and luck.

Materials: A deck of cards.

Process: One member is the dealer. He or she deals two cards to each player, including self. One card is dealt face up and the other face down. Players look at the card which is up and decide if they want more cards. The dealer gives cards in turn to each player who wants one. The object is to get the cards to add up to 21 without going over. (King, queen, and jack equal 10 points; ace is either 1 or 11.)

Adaptations: Patients who are not secure with the game can play with a buddy. A more complex game is Uno, which allows form matching, sequencing, and reversing orders. A less complex card game which requires less energy from the members is Old Maid, which involves simple matching.

Going on a Trip

Purpose: To increase interaction and memory (good filler when waiting for another game to be set up or as a transition to wrap-up).

Materials: None.

Process: Patients may be spread out informally around the room. The leader explains that this game involves pretending to go on a trip, and everyone gets to name one thing they'd like to take. The leader starts and each person repeats what is previously listed before adding his or her own item. For instance, "I'm going on a trip and I'm going to take a suitcase." The next person says, "I'm going on a trip and I'm going to take a suitcase and a camera." The game continues until everyone has a turn.

Adaptations: The game can start over after a set number of items to remember, such as every fourth turn. A specific kind of trip can be named, such as camping or going to the beach.

Pass the Can (Modified Charades)

Purpose: To improve nonverbal communication skills and enhance interaction through guessing each person's movement.

Materials: Can, music, movement cards.

Process: The leaders make up cards which have instructions for movement, such as, "Pretend you are blowing a bubble," "Act as if you are ironing a shirt," "Make your face look as though you are eating a lemon." The members pass the can around the circle as the music plays. When the music stops, the person holding the can draws a card and reads the instructions silently. Then he or she acts out the instruction and the group tries to guess what the person is imitating. Start the music and repeat procedures.

Adaptations: To make the game very safe, a rule is built in that members have the option not to act out the card on their turn.

To make the game more enticing, patients can receive chips. For example, reading the card gets one chip, acting it out gets two. At the end of the game they can be traded in for a treat, such as a small balloon, a blue ribbon, or piece of gum.

The cards can be graded to include more complex activities, organized by themes (hobbies, action movie titles, types of work).

Crafts

(Most materials available from S&S Arts and Crafts Catalog)

Bead Necklaces

Purpose: To encourage fine motor coordination, frustration tolerance, and sense of self through completion of a task; the finished product can be worn.

Materials: Assorted beads (e.g., giant seed beads, oval beads, and separated beads), elastic cord, scissors, and cups to put beads in.

Process: Materials are arranged on table for each member. Choices are offered regarding size of elastic (necklace or bracelet) and colors and shapes of beads. Beading is demonstrated by the co-leaders.

Adaptations: Discussion is on who would like it, when to wear it, and comparing this type of craft with others.

Adult Designs to Color

Purpose: To increase concentration, decision-making, fine motor coordination, and sense of accomplishment through completion of a task.

Materials: Thin markers and adult designs from S&S catalog, such as Art Nouveau Windows, Easy Way Pictures, Jungle Families, Still Lives and Scenes, and Pretty Posies.

Process: Patients are given several designs from which to choose one to color. Other choices are offered regarding size of poster, colors to use, and amount to complete.

Adaptations: Pens can be set up at a parallel level with everyone having a set, but usually at a more interactive level with some available for sharing and passing. Patients can do a second picture or help someone else if they get done quicker than the rest of the group.

Discussion often focuses on quiet v. active activities, preference for structure v. free form, and neat v. messy art media, knowing when to stop (not overcoloring) for the best effect, art for relaxation without feeling a pressure to be artistic, and being able to complete a task.

Teapot Memo Pad

Purpose: To encourage following directions, deciding what to do with a practical project, and experiencing pleasure through accomplishment.

Materials: Memo pad kit, glue. Optional: Ink stamps with designs and stamp pads.

Process: Members select a colored calico precut fabric, piece of wood, and pad of paper. Fabric is glued to the wood, right side up. Cardboard back of paper is glued to fabric.

Adaptations: Those who do not find the project challenging or who finish quicker may decorate each piece of paper with an inkstamp design.

Discussion focuses on what to use it for, where to keep it, if they would rather give it as a present and if so, to whom, and other projects they have made recently or in the past.

Mugs to Decorate

Purpose: To reinforce identity through writing one's name on a personal object.

Materials: Plastic mugs with removable paper, marking pens from Nasco Arts and Crafts, 901 Janesville Avenue, Ft. Atkinson, WI 53538; (414) 563-2446.

Process: Members are given a mug and a piece of paper. They write their names and decorate the paper. Then the paper is placed in the plastic covering.

Adaptations: A short project, it gives immediate success. Can prolong involvement by planning to drink juice from the mug and discuss when members will use mug. May want to have everyone make two mugs, one for themselves and one for a gift. Also, can allow for more creativity in designing pictures on the mug.

Decoupage Plaques or Key Chains

Purpose: To encourage following instructions, a sense of accomplishment, and frustration tolerance through task completion.

Materials: Wood plaques, designs, mod podge, brushes, cups of water.

Process: Materials are arranged on table for each member. Choices are offered regarding size of plaque and design. Instructions are written on board and discussed verbally with a demonstration of how to brush on mod podge (used as both a glue and varnish).

Adaptations: Key chains can provide a smaller, more practical project. Discussion is on where to keep projects, who else would enjoy having one, and how people feel about their accomplishments.

Leather Stamping Key Chains

Purpose: To encourage fine motor and eye-hand coordination with tools, following instructions, decision-making, and frustration tolerance through task accomplishment.

Materials: Leather key fobs, key chains, margarine cups filled with water, stamping tools, wood mallets, little sponges, and stains.

Process: Materials are arranged on table for each member. Choices are offered regarding stamping designs and color of stain. Instructions are written on the board and discussed verbally with a demonstration of how to stamp, and later how to apply stain.

Adaptations: Stamping designs may include initials, animals, and assorted shapes. Attention must be given to orienting the stamps in the correct direction. Discussion is on working with leather, using key chains, and having responsibilities.

Copper Tooling Coaster

Purpose: To encourage fine motor coordination, following directions, and frustration tolerance through task completion.

Materials: Pieces of copper, plastic molds, soft clay, masking tape, steel wool, wood dowels, wood coasters.

Process: Materials are arranged on table for each member. Choices are offered regarding designs. Instructions are written on the board and discussed verbally with a demonstration of how to use the wood dowels to make the design appear on the copper. Co-leaders help patients put masking tape around edges, for safety, and clay in finished mold.

Adaptations: Small plaques may be used instead. Discussion is on copper tooling as a craft, use of coasters, and sense of satisfaction from completing projects.

Tissue Paper Flowers

Purpose: To encourage fine motor coordination, following instructions, decision-making, frustration tolerance, and sense of accomplishment through task completion.

Materials: Assorted colors of tissue paper, scissors, and pipe cleaners.

Process: Materials are arranged on table for each member. Choices are offered regarding color and size of flowers. Paper is cut for first flower about the size of a facial tissue. Four to six layers of paper are placed on top of each other. Co-leader demonstrates how to make half-inch accordion folds. Pipe cleaner is wrapped around folds at the center and is held onto while separating layers of tissues. Starting at edges, tissues are gently pulled apart until they resemble a flower. Longer pipe cleaner can be attached for stem.

Adaptations: Members can keep flowers for themselves or contribute some for ward party decorations. Discussion is on the project itself, decorations, and keeping things v. giving them away.

Mobile — God's Eyes or Wind Chimes

Purpose: To encourage fine motor coordination, frustration tolerance, and sense of accomplishment through task completion.

Materials: Yarns, wood dowels, and instructions from S&S catalog. Circle shells, paint, brushes, strings, and dowels from S&S Philippine Wind Chimes kit.

Process: Materials are arranged on table for each member. Choices regarding colors are offered. Wood dowels are preattached by co-leaders, who demonstrate how to wind yarn around dowels. Co-leaders help patients tie off ends when done.

Adaptations: Decorations are tied to string for individual mobile or tied together for a group mobile. Mobile can be made from shell wind chimes instead, with members decorating each shell with paint.

Discussion is on uses of mobiles, appeal of different designs, and individual v. group projects.

Block Printing Greeting Cards

Purpose: To encourage creativity, sensitivity for others, and sense of accomplishment through task completion.

Materials: Blank greeting cards, envelopes, markers, stencils, and pencils.

Process: Materials are arranged on table for each member. Choices regarding design and purpose of card are offered. Stencils of common objects, such as hearts, flowers, and stars, are prepared. Members are encouraged to plan who to make a card for and decide on the occasion. Ideas are discussed with the group as needed. Members decorate their cards. They make as many as time allows.

Adaptations: More complex designs can be made by some members, including adding collage materials (magazine pictures, glue, scissors). Discussion is on giving and getting, and homemade things v. commercial.

Sand Terrariums

Purpose: To encourage creativity, fine motor coordination, and frustration tolerance through task completion.

Materials: Assorted colored stands, cups for pouring, clear plastic cups for terrarium, wood dowels.

Process: Materials are arranged on table for each member. Choices regarding color and design are offered. Co-leader demonstrates pouring and designing technique with the dowel. Patients are assisted as needed.

Adaptations: Terrariums can be more complex by adding cuttings from plants and potting them in dirt on top of the sand. Discussion is on crafts at art fairs, taking care of plants, and doing something new.

Monthly Calendar

Purpose: To assist with orientation to time, contributing to a group project, and interaction around a task.

Materials: Large poster board, construction paper, glue, tape, markers, ruler, pencil, and scissors.

Process: Prior to group the co-leaders prepare a large calendar on the poster board with blank spaces for each day of the month. A theme for the month is planned with a large decoration next to the poster and construction paper designs — one for each day (e.g., for March, a large Snoopy holding shamrocks, and precut green four-leaf clovers for the days).

Glue and markers are placed on the table for sharing. Either the co-leader or a higher functioning patient within the group helps the members decide who will write which numbers on the precut construction paper designs. The numbers and members' names are written on the blackboard for assistance. Each member writes with the marker the assigned numbers, one on each form. The numbers are attached to the calendar in order with masking tape. Discussion is on special days during the month, such as birthdays, holidays, discharges, planned weekend activities.

Adaptations: A highly gradable task. A lower functioning group can be assigned numbers in sequence. A higher functioning group can be given stencils to trace and cut out the construction paper designs. They could also make a cardboard arrow which is pointed to the day of the month. In a mixed group the more organized patients can decorate their precut forms, help others, and assist with putting the finished forms on the calendar. Care must be taken with at-risk patients to monitor scissor use. Moving the arrow each day is a special role for a low functioning patient.

Mural

Purpose: To encourage participation in a group project, stimulate expression of interests, and involvement in a creative task.

Materials: Large piece of mural paper, pencils, markers, paints, brushes, and cups for water.

Process: For a cohesive group, the members plan a common theme for the mural and divide up the sections each individual will do, either by content or space (e.g., a patient may do a tree or whatever is needed in his or her area).

Adaptations: Highly gradable. To begin to create the experience of a group project, co-leaders can divide space with lines, like frames on a movie film. Co-leaders decide on a theme, such as Christmas, and outline the beginning of an object in each frame, such as a tree, a star, or a candy cane. Then the patients take a frame and embellish the drawing, adding ornaments, ribbons, and so on. At the end the members can see they helped create the group mural.

A little more challenging level would be to have the patients draw on one frame for a few minutes, then rotate everyone to the next frame. This gives patients the experience of contributing to something in addition to their own work. Patients can try different media, from markers to paints.

Instead of a mural, a wallhanging can be devised using collage as the medium. The main part of the project can be precut, for example, a Christmas wreath out of felt, and the patients can use stencils to cut pine cones, bells, and bows. The co-leaders need to analyze this complex task to provide sufficient structure for the range of needs and levels of functioning in the group.

Wrap-up Activities

List Activities of the Session
Purpose: To review sequence of events and enhance short-term memory.
Materials: Blackboard, eraser, and chalk.
Process: Co-leader asks the patients what they did in the session today. He or she writes them so that they can be placed in the order they were done. Then patients are asked to raise their hands for the one they liked the best. It's fine if patients raise their hands for more than one; then the discussion of interests can be encouraged.
Adaptations: Elaborate on interests by structuring the voting. Make columns next to the activities and write the number of votes for each question. For example, "How many people would like to do the activity again?" "Which activities were the hardest?"

Good, Better, Best
Purpose: To encourage self-report about pleasure from activities and interactions.
Materials: Blackboard, eraser, and chalk.
Process: At the end of the group ask how people feel now compared with when they first came into the session. Make three columns for "good" (or "same"), "better," and "best" (since they have been in hospital). Not exactly parallel construction, but they will get the idea!
Adaptations: Change labels! Elaborate on in what ways they feel differently and why that might be. Ask what could they do to feel better in the next session.

Guess What
Purpose: To encourage decision-making, verbal participation, and initiative.
Materials: Blackboard, eraser, and chalk.
Process: Co-leader asks the group questions and writes the answers on the board. For instance, Guess what was the most active game today? Guess what was the longest category during the balloon game? Guess what day tomorrow is?
Adaptations: Co-leaders can bail each other out if they get stuck. Even though one person is at the board, the others can suggest questions.

Guess Who
Purpose: To encourage attention to members of the group and the roles they took.
Materials: Blackboard, eraser, and chalk.
Process: Similar to Guess What. Ask questions, such as, Guess who was the first person to come to group today? Guess who is wearing street clothes for the first time? Guess who was funny during the balloon volleyball game? Guess who is leaving the group tomorrow?
Adaptations: The co-leaders can bring up graded questions intending

	○ Low	◐ Medium	● High
Energy Level	Passive	Average for group Somewhat alert, some spontaneous movement	Hyperactive

Skills:

	Low	Medium	High
Gross Motor	One motion-repeated Sit to stand	Range of motion Basic throwing	More complicated movements/coordination
Fine Motor	Grasp	Pinch (Brush strokes)	Writing, Drawing, Tool use
Perceptual Motor	Stimulation of senses	Perceive up/down, Basic movement relationships, Figure-ground	Read, Write, Right/Left discrimination, Back/front More complex spatial relationships
Cognitive (Process)	One direction, Matching SImple memory	Rules, Figuring out part of game/activity, Choices	Planning, Scoring
Interaction	Parallel, Eye contact, Doing activities at same time	A little talking as part of the game/activity	Simple conversation, Basic self-disclosure
Preparation	One item (on hand) Just blackboard or chairs required	Need to order supplies Prepare within 15 min. before group	More than 15 min. required

Needs
1 = Active involvement
2 = Attention to meaning
3 = Fun
4 = Interaction
5 = Interests
6 = Longer activity
7 = Movement
8 = Self-expression
9 = Slow pace
10 = Solve problems (cognitive challenge)
11 = Structure - follow instructions
12 = Value - as group member

Table A-2. Key to List of Analyzed Activities

them for specific patients to answer. In this way patients can contribute at their own level. Attention to the individual goals also needs to be emphasized during this section of the group by giving patients an opportunity to make one comment, listen so that others can speak, and so forth.

Which Skills

Purpose: To help patients learn to be their own occupational therapist and analyze the skills required to perform daily activities.

Materials: Blackboard, eraser, and chalk.

Process: After listing the activities of the session, patients are asked what skills they used. The co-leader might give an example, such as concentration

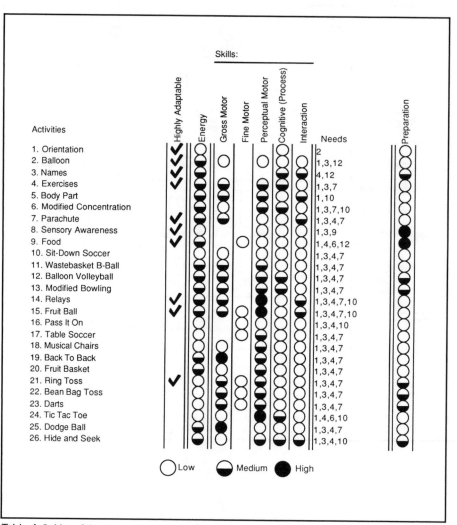

Table A-3. List of Analyzed Activites.

during the alphabet game, and then ask what other skills were necessary to play that game. Patients are surprisingly able to identify skills correctly.

Adaptations: If patients really seem to get the concept, then you can generalize to activities they do outside of the hospital. For example, "What skills did you use in this group that you also need in your daily routine when you leave here?"

Individual Goals

Purpose: To acknowledge individual goals for group members, increase members' awareness of each other's goals, and facilitate achievement of goals.

Materials: Cards with individual goals written on them, star stickers, or a poster with members' names and goals.

Process: During the weekly co-leaders meeting for Directive Group, iden-

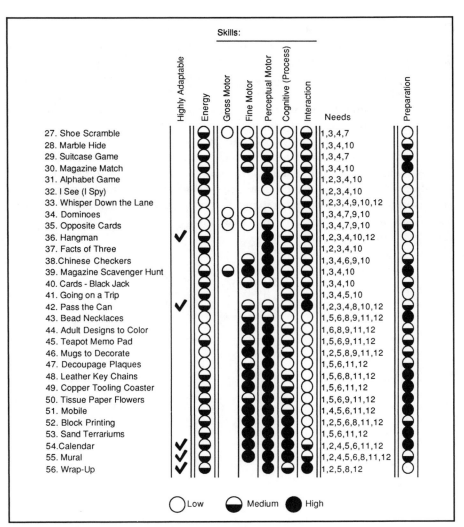

Table A-3. List of Analyzed Activites *(continued)*

tify a goal for each patient and write his or her name and the goal on a large note card. At the beginning of the group, hand out the cards. Have each member introduce him or herself and read the goal. At the end of the session, discuss whether members obtained their goals. Give and solicit specific feedback about when behavior was observed or how the behavior could be implemented in the future. Stickers can be given to those who demonstrated progress toward reaching their goals.

Adaptations: Make a poster listing everyone's name and goal. At the end of the group, check off those that met their goal. If five columns are drawn, this can be done each day of the week. However, a balance between rigidity in the routine and attention to goals needs to be reached. The poster does not need to be institutionalized any more than cards or stickers.

Graduation Awards/Certificates of Participation

Purpose: To acknowledge individual achievement, reinforce obtainment of group goals, and enhance self-esteem (personal causation).

Materials: Award certificates and ribbons from S&S catalog or give hand-made ones.

Process: When patients are ready to leave the group, they get a graduation award stating they have met the goals of Directive Group.

Adaptations: Additional awards can be given to other members for progress towards work on individual goals, such as staying in the group for the entire session, leading one activity, or making an activity suggestion.

Patients who have plateaued may also be discharged from the group. They are given a certificate of participation to emphasize the achievements they have made to date. They are leaving the group to try other ways to work on their goals outside of the group.

INDEX

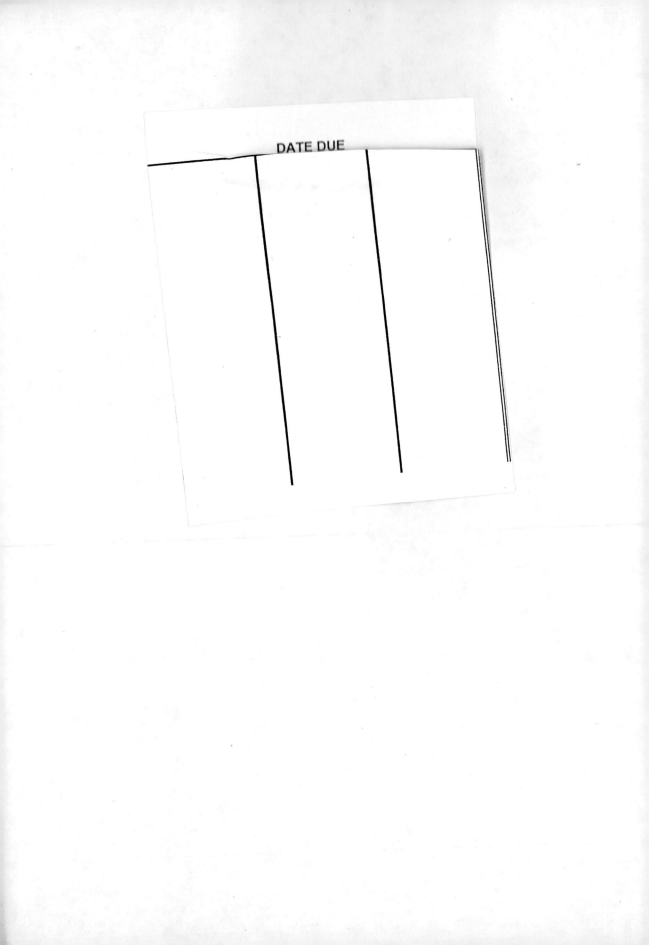

DATE DUE